VANISHING TRIBES

VANISHING TRIBES

PRIMITIVE MAN ON EARTH

Alain Chenevière

A DOLPHIN BOOK

DOUBLEDAY & COMPANY, INC.

GARDEN CITY, NEW YORK

1987

To my son, Alexandre

ARTISTIC DIRECTOR: Eric Tschumi
TRANSLATION: Marjorie de Roquemaurel
PRINTING: Dai Nippon, Tokyo

Library of Congress Cataloging-in-Publication Data

Chenevière, Alain.
Vanishing tribes.

"A Dolphin book."
1. Ethnology. 2. Tales. 3. Native races.
4. Acculturation. I. Title.
GN380.C48 1987   306   86-29047
ISBN 0-385-23897-5

CONTENTS

INTRODUCTION

by Elizabeth Antébi

Who hasn't dreamed of seeking adventure in distant lands, among strange peoples totally different from what one has known before? Who hasn't imagined himself as an adventurer—a Marco Polo or a medieval knight? Within the pages of this book, one's dreams can come true . . .

Alain Chenevière is a linguist and ethnologist. Through his work he introduces us to men, women and children who still live as they did at the dawn of civilization, among gods and spirits. He speaks of their migrations, their customs and beliefs. Alain Chenevière is also a photographer. His presence among the peoples who adopted him (in some cases literally) became so familiar as to be ignored. His pictures show them as they are, not as they might be persuaded to pose for strangers. Chenevière is also fascinated by legends. Endowed with a prodigious memory, he has transcribed for the first time tribal myths which until now were transmitted only orally from generation to generation.

This book is the final result of a long mission, the mission of a man who for more than twenty years lived with over two hundred vanishing tribes from the jungles of Borneo to the banks of the river Omo. It was a mission fraught with danger: encountering the hostility of military authorities who forbade access to strategic regions; bribing smugglers (whose rule of life is "nothing given, nothing gained"); confronting the menacing threats of arms traffickers and persuading them to accept him as a passenger on their boats.

Alain Chenevière took on his quest in the image of the "Great Serpent," a poetical myth which encompasses elements common to a number of tribal legends throughout the world. The Great Serpent, as legend goes, traveled around the earth, laying as he went the eggs from which hatched the legends of all the tribes. He foresaw, however, the coming of the Last Morning of the World, a calamity resulting from man's failure to preserve the equilibrium in nature. This is the legend of The Great Serpent:

At the very beginning of time, there was nothing but nonexistence.

The first god, who existed long before the fathers of the great gods began to shine in the heavens, drew an endless line through the original void. The line extended, invisibly and intangibly, into infinity.

Stars and planets already inhabited the skies but the line was there, concealed.

Earth appeared. The line was there, silent and patient.

Water gushed forth. The line was there, mysterious and pure.

Fire sparked. The line was there, waiting and ready.

The four primordial elements began rotating in a vast circular movement.

***Earth,** first of all, took its place under the line and blazed a long, deep trail in the universe.*

***Water** flowed into the furrow, giving it volume and curves.*

***Air,** in turn, seized an extremity of the new entity and carried it off to the top of the world, transforming it into a bridge connecting what is on high to what is below.*

***Fire,** finally, illuminated every part of what the other elements had created, endowing it with eternal youth, purity and magic.*

From nonexistence arose existence. The original serpent had been born.

It lived, and within it lived the four elements, all antagonists united for the first time.

The serpent-god then began to slither through the heavens, drawing in his wake the universe with all its stars and planets . . . time was set in motion, and the world began to rotate. The eggs laid by the serpent-god gave birth to legends. The serpent-god moved on. Worlds appeared and disappeared; he kept moving. Various beings lived, then perished; he moved ever on.

The rule was that everything that disappeared should be replaced by a new creation.

However, our fathers' fathers' fathers had predicted that the serpent-god's advance would slow down because of man, that the four elements would eventually separate and endanger the universe with destruction.

A little while ago, man separated the earth from the other elements and the earth said, "I have created the strongest beings, I deserve to rule!"

A little while ago, man separated water from the other elements and the water said, "I have given birth to the most intelligent beings, I deserve to rule!"

A little while ago, man separated air from the other elements and the air said, "I have nurtured the most courageous beings, I deserve to rule!"

A little while ago, man separated fire from the other elements and the fire said, "I have created the purest beings, I deserve to rule!"

The serpent-god then slackened his pace.

As he looked at the four primordial forces, he said that they could only live in union. He wept over the misfortune that would destroy the universe if there were dissension among them. Then the thought came to him:

Earth, water, air and fire, you are the beginning of everything, but you are also the end. I exist through you and you exist in me. Together, we have been present at the morning of the world; if our unity is broken, we will see the last morning of the world.

"All of the tribes represented in this book," says Alain Chenevière, "and over three hundred others, are sooner or later condemned to death, victims of the modern world. Annihilated by those who massacre them in the name of Allah with promises of Paradise, harassed by missionaries who try to explain to a Papou cannibal that Jesus died for him two thousand years ago in a distant land called Palestine, these tribes are also victims of oil prospectors, highway and dam constructors, miners of precious

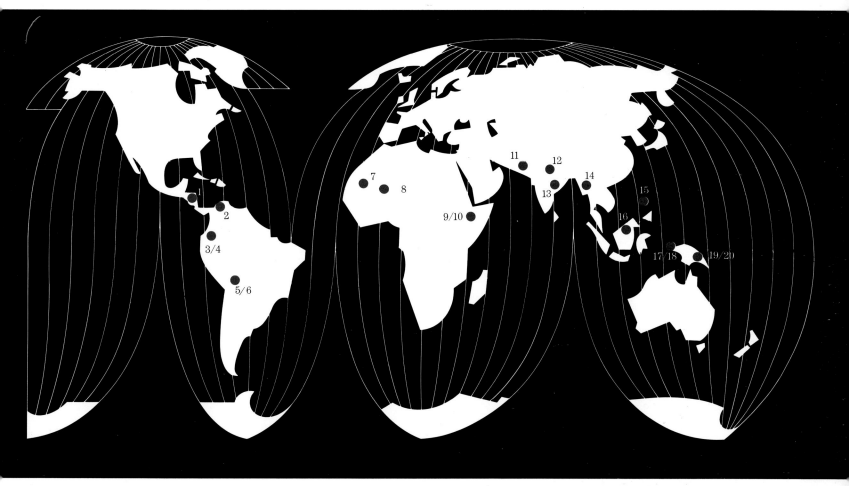

Geographical Locations of the Tribes in This Book

1. Cuna (Panama)
2. Kogi (Colombia)
3. Colorados (Ecuador)
4. Warani (Ecuador)
5. Chipaya (Bolivia)
6. Tarabuqueños (Bolivia)
7. N'madi (Mauritania)

8. Dogon (Mali)
9. Mursi (Ethiopia)
10. Kara-Hamar (Ethiopia)
11. Kalash (Pakistan)
12. Ladakh-pa (Tibet)
13. Bonda (India)
14. Akha (Burma-Thailand-Laos)

15. Ifugao (Philippines)
16. Punan (Borneo)
17. Asmat (Irian Jaya)
18. Jale (Irian Jaya)
19. Medlpa (Papua, New Guinea)
20. Washkuk (Papua, New Guinea)

stones or strategic metals, drug traffickers, Marxist guerrillas, ruthless dictators and political idealists who dream of a world in which all peoples are alike."

Vanishing Tribes is an homage not only to these doomed peoples, but to ancestral wisdom in its sacred sense, to respect for the laws of the universe which, like the tribes, are in danger of vanishing from human memory. Some of the peoples, like the Warani and the N'madi, have almost completely disappeared. Alain Chenevière is not merely attacking the values of the Western world, however. He lives here, and without our modern technical achievements these photographs would never have been taken. He is, simply, amazed and often outraged by the blind determination of those who are attempting to "civilize" these peoples whose way of life, environment and beliefs are totally different from those of modern societies which try to assimilate them by substituting science for folklore, materialism for magic, or, to quote Chenevière, "to destroy their multicolored universe by imposing our one-dimensional world of black and white."

These tribes are dying with dignity, nobility and courage. Trustees of the secrets of an entirely different civilization, they refuse to forsake their gods and ancestral spirits. Few deplore their destinies; fewer still sense that it may well foreshadow the twilight of our own civilizations.

Alain Chenevière has selected twenty tribes to be represented in his "family album." These he feels are representative of them all. Their selection was not an easy task; in the end it was made in his heart.

Behind these words and pictures one can see the quest of a man impassioned by what he calls "different people." Chenevière is a man who chose a life of adventure, exploring hostile and perilous regions in order to acquaint us with these peoples threatened by extinction.

Born right after World War II, Alain Chenevière was raised in the Far East. His first meeting with peoples who were "different" occurred when he was thirteen. While on a trip with friends of his parents, he heard about a mysterious mountain tribe living on the frontier of Afghanistan and Pakistan, so he hopped on his bicycle one day and sought them out. They shared their meals with him and he found himself happy in their midst. He never would forget the joy he felt during his first brief escapade.

With a remarkable gift for languages, he was trilingual as a child, then studied Latin, Greek and Sanskrit. He later picked up an understanding of numerous dialects, even learning to speak some of them. His father, a passionate voyager and scholar, took him to Olympia, Sumer, Egypt and Turkey and he also gave him his first camera. "I started out," says Alain Chenevière, "by photographing old stones. The gods had lived among them! Where Troy once stood (although no trace remains), I felt the ancients' presence along with invisible shades of the past. When I began traveling in South America, Thailand, Indonesia, I continually photographed the people who lived among the old stones."

Between his voyages, Alain Chenevière acquired a master's degree in Indo-European grammar at the University of Lyons. He then passed the examination which entitled him to teach that subject. All during this time he continued to pursue the trail of the Great Serpent and record the legends of the tribal peoples who still lived among the gods.

In the Andes, he visited tribes which even the ruthless conquistadors had been unable to conquer. They taught him the secrets of the virgin forest, how to detect and follow a trail, to scent the wind, to hunt game, and how to identify a vague shape in the distance: Was it a giant orchid or preying beast?

Among the Papous he returned to the Stone Age: ritual chants, stone hatchets, and fire produced by rubbing together sticks of wood or bits of flint. It became an incredible experience of regression in time.

With the Ethiopians of the Omo Valley, he was dazzled by the bodily perfection of these magnificent giants—giants so fragile that their bones could shatter like glass at the slightest impact.

In the heart of Asia, he marveled at the refinement of the art and culture, the garments and adornments of the Akha and Ladakhi women.

With the Punan and the Asmat, he first experienced tribal adoption rites. "At the beginning of my visit to the Asmat, I slept in the ceremonial hut, abode of spirits and ancestral ghosts. Gradually, though, the men permitted me to join in their activities. I paddled alongside them down the river, hunted with them, helped plant and harvest taro and sweet potatoes, played with their children, went about unclothed as they did. They finally accepted me as one of them. They taught me to wield arrows, track game, distinguish edible berries and fruit from poisonous varieties. Then one day I was given a "hunting father," who led me before the Council of Elders. A certain family wished to adopt me officially; the ceremony would take place at the next new moon. They made no demands, posed no conditions, nor did I ask anything of them; it was a natural event that simply occurred."

Ritual adoption of this kind is rare, practiced only among peoples most menaced by extinction. It is a means of strengthening a tribe struggling for survival in a hostile environment. The Punan and Asmat live in isolated settlements in the heart of the jungle. Chenevière helped them by providing useful presents of arrowheads, medicine and nylon thread. Other tribes had no reason to adopt him. "With the Colorados, for example, my bonds of friendship were just as strong, but they live on the outskirts of a modern city where they can easily procure whatever they need. I was always considered a guest, a friend, but still part of the civilized world and not of the tribe."

Avidly curious to discover new ways of life, learn new customs and hear more legends, Alain Chenevière was surprised by the lack of interest tribal members showed in the world from which he came. When they asked him questions, they simply would not understand his replies. For example, one day an important chief of the Kogi in Colombia led him to his village and introduced him to his son. "What is your name?" asked Chenevière. "Pedro," replied the child. "But what is your Kogi name?" "Ah, I said Pedro so that you'd understand. My real name is Wichi." When Alain Chenevière returned to visit the Kogi, his own son had been born. The chief's son asked him what his son's name was. "Alexandre," said Chenevière. "Not that one," said the child, "I want to know his real name."

There is no magic formula for discovering and making friends with "different" people. Alain Chenevière believes that one must simply abandon one's habits and prejudices. He also feels that he himself is protected by a benevolent star and was somehow predestined to be recognized as one of them by their chiefs and sorcerers. It is not his intention to reveal the secrets of these tribes or the mysteries of life lived in a different dimension from ours. He simply wants to show us how to see and hear what has become invisible and inaudible to us. His lucky star is still leading him toward other lands and other primitive tribes.

"Wherever I may be, I live in constant anticipation of departure, and regret for what I am about to leave behind. My destiny is to discover other magic places, other different people, and to follow the trail of the Great Serpent which steadily wends its way toward the Last Morning of the World."

MEDLPA

Papua, New Guinea

The Medlpa are a belligerent people of imposing stature, well over six feet tall, descended from Negroid populations that invaded Melanesia some ten thousand years ago. They remained isolated in the mountains of New Guinea, uncontaminated by other strains, until 1930 when gold was discovered near the town of Morobe. When the white man arrived, he pushed ever farther west in search of the precious metal, until he came in contact with the Medlpa.

Warfare was a permanent traditional activity of this vengeful and aggressive tribe. Even though armed combat has been outlawed by the Australian government as well as by the independent Papou administration, the mountain region the Medlpa inhabit is still the scene of frequent battles between various clans.

The family clan is the basic unit of the Medlpa social structure. They live in secluded houses rather than in villages. The patriarch and initiated men reside in quarters separate from those of non-initiated boys, women and children, who share their dwelling with the pigs. There is no disgrace in this; pigs are treated as companions, almost members of the family, often breast-fed by women. They are rarely killed to be eaten, only on certain feast days. The clans are very close-knit, their vigor maintained by continuous ritual exchanges. A new member of a clan adopts its causes and quarrels, shares its debts and honors. If a member of a clan is in danger, all the others immediately come to his defense.

Their principal festival, the *moka* (called *tee* by the Engs in the south, *sing-sing* by the whites), was originally a gathering of adversaries at the end of a war to decide on reparations due. Since the official abolition of tribal warfare, it has become a more peaceful means of expressing rivalry and belligerence among the clans. They vie with one another to determine which is most adept at simulated combat, most gorgeously adorned, most terrifyingly masked, and which can offer the most magnificent gifts. The proceedings sometimes still degenerate into genuine battle with lances, "head-crackers," bows and arrows, and even revolvers, so that many deaths result.

The "big man" of each clan is elected by the Council of Elders, and is responsible for organizing the *moka* and financing it. His honor and entire future are at stake. In the case of victory, he is allowed to join the Council of Elders and enjoys great esteem; in the case of defeat, he loses face and may even be chased out of the community.

Daily life is devoted to agriculture, strictly divided between the sexes. Men clear the surface of the land and plant banana trees and sugarcane, which yield fruit that grows above the ground. Cultivating underground plants such as taro and sweet potatoes is reserved for the women.

Warfare, agriculture, and family and clan matters are their principal preoccupations.

The Arms of the Ancestor

Long ago, the earth was covered with vast forests inhabited by few men and many animals. Nikint and Pakla were two expert hunters who belonged to enemy clans. Both had been tracking the same deer for a long time. The deer fell to the ground, mortally wounded by both their arrows. The hunters eyed each other, ready for combat. Then they burst out laughing and decided to share the spoils. They were friends from that day on. They built a house, then divided the game they had bagged. They acquired lots of pigs and fertile land. They often laughed and always hunted together, until one day their paths happened to diverge. When they met that evening, Nikint was the first to speak: "Pakla, my friend, see the beautiful fruit I found in the forest. It was on a tree and I cut off a branch. I will plant it and we will have wonderful fruit." Pakla replied, "Nikint, my friend, see the beautiful sweet potato I found in the forest. It was growing underneath some shrubs and I dug up a root. I will plant it and we will have wonderful sweet potatoes."

And so they both did as they said. The branch became a tree which multiplied and bore much fruit. The root became a plant which multiplied and bore many sweet potatoes. But the time came when the two friends no longer wished to share their harvests, each one claiming that he did more work than the other and that all the benefit should be his. They quarreled, insulted each other and even came to blows—but the memory of their past friendship stopped them. They decided to separate. It was agreed that Nikint would remain where they were and Pakla would leave. In compensation, Pakla asked Nikint to give him something of value. Nikint handed him weapons that he himself had made: a lance, a bow and arrows. Pakla set forth and had many mishaps and adventures.

One day, tired and hungry, Pakla came upon a little garden filled with taro and sweet potatoes. As there was no one in sight, he scaled the fence and satisfied his hunger, then fell asleep. When he awoke, the owner of the field was seated in front of him, observing him. Pakla thought his final hour had come—the man was surely going to kill him. On the contrary, the stranger, without a word, pointed to a straw pallet and invited Pakla to rest. But he fell only half asleep. The next day the man returned. By gestures, he made Pakla understand that he should weed the garden, which Pakla did. That evening the man brought him food. The following day Pakla had to care for the pigs; the next day, gather the fruit. Then he repaired the fence, cultivated the sweet potatoes, cleared the earth, ground the taro. Each evening he received a meal from the man, who had not yet uttered a word.

One morning, when the sun was already high in the sky, the man was late in coming. Pakla was beginning to worry when the man arrived, leading a young girl by the hand. For the first time he spoke. "My name is Epone Kuma. I have watched you and know that you are strong and brave. I have no children. But here is Mande, the daughter of my brother who was killed at war. I give her to you as your wife so that you will no longer be alone." Overjoyed by the idea of founding a family, Pakla eagerly accepted. Sons were born. He taught them to carve weapons. In memory of his old friendship, he told them always to fashion their weapons exactly like the lance, bow and arrows that his old friend Nikint had made and given him. His sons obeyed him. They in turn had sons who founded the Wabag tribe. Their weapons, as Pakla had wished, were in all details identical with the ones Nikint had given him.

One day the Wabags encountered men from the Laïagam tribe and a war broke out between them. It lasted a long time. During every battle, a strange phenomenon occurred: the arrows and lances of the Laïagams killed the Wabags, while the Wabags' shots missed the Laïagam warriors or barely scratched them. They finally made a truce. When they began to talk about their founding ancestors, the Wabags learned that the Laïagams were descended from the sons of Nikint. Then they understood! They understood that their weapons, descendants of those of Nikint, would never be willing to kill the descendants of the sons of Nikint. How could the father's weapons slay his own sons? Just as Pakla and Nikint had done when they were friends, they all burst out laughing.

Since that time, during the *moka* rites, the Laïagams' chants commemorate and preserve the memory of the battles in which the Wabag arrows could not harm them because Nikint had offered in fond friendship his lance, bow and arrows to Pakla.

1. *Most of the farmlands are situated in the valleys (here in the region of Kindarib), where sweet potatoes, maize and, since about 1970, coffee are grown—the latter representing a useful source of income.*

2. *The houses are built on the mountaintops (here in the region of Jambul), an easier position to defend in time of war.*

3,4. *In remote regions, guards still watch over the paths leading to the villages. Black face paint, symbolizing strength in combat, is often combined with white-dyed beards, symbolic of ancestral wisdom. The crescent-shaped pendant (kina) is carved from the lip of a pearl oyster. It indicates that for the*

1

2

3

traditional ceremonial celebrations, the wearer has been a munificent donor. It is symbolic of victory over an enemy tribe to give more than one receives (pigs, feathers, weapons). The kina was long the only form of monetary exchange. Even today, when New Guinea has official currency (also called kina), the shell retains its value in many regions. The strange headdresses of the Medlpa are made from the hair they save from their infancy each time it is cut.

5,6. Unlike other tribes who group together in large villages in the central mountains, the Medlpa live in isolated family homes.

4

5

6

Preparing for a moka *near Jibulge.*
1. The man is carrying the ceremonial stone hatchet called a tinggrina. *His companion is covering his legs with a white paste made from roots which have been pounded and mixed with clay.*

2,3. Ocher is obtained from clay, while black is a mixture of charcoal and cinders diluted in water and grease. Bright colors formerly obtained from natural products such as fruits and plants are today replaced by

1

2

artificial colorings bought from itinerant vendors or in shops. The woman here (2) is wearing the fur and tail of the kuskus, a small marsupial.

4. For the duration of the moka, the wives of deceased chieftains lead the clan in place of their defunct husbands, in accordance with traditional laws. As a sign of their temporary function, they wear a half gourd on their chest.

3

4

1,2,5. The women's faces, painted to give a mask effect, always have a background of red, symbolizing the fertility of the feminine sex. Red also symbolizes friendly communication between the clans and sexes.

1

2

3

4

5

3,4,6,7. *Men, whose duty it is to inspire terror in their enemies, wear black masks which they try to make even more frightful by painting grotesque patterns around the eyes and on the nose. Some warriors (7) anoint their body with tinted oil made from ashes and melted lard, stick wild boar horns in their nose, or cover themselves with moss and leaves. They thus become "plant men," in contact with the forest spirits and endowed with supernatural powers. Some* kina *are enhanced by being mounted on a plaque of resin powdered with ocher and worn upon the chest (3).*

6

7

1

1,2. Leaves and feathers constitute the base of the costume. Among the latter, feathers of birds of paradise, cockatoos, parrots, and King of Saxony are highly valued, especially those from the King of Saxony bird of paradise because they are used in the decoration of the koi wal, *the highest-ranking headdress very tall and multicolored.*

2. In the course of the morl *dance the participants bend their knees to the rhythm of the drums, their long grass aprons swaying in unison with their feathered headdresses. The*

2

line they form, called a kanan, is an important aspect in the moka ritual because it shows the solidarity of the clan's warriors.

3. The spider designs, called "teardrops," which appear only on the feminine masks, are intended to emphasize the features of the face, thus bringing out its grace and beauty.

4. The "Big Man," at left, verifies the rank of his clan. To assure their victory during moka, he frequently incurs great debts. In return, he gets many privileges: he is the uncontested arbiter of disputes within his clan; his land is cultivated by other members of the tribe; and he has the right to take several wives—a custom which is progressively disappearing under the influence of missionaries.

5,6. Whereas the young man wears a restrained headdress, the chief proudly parades the koi wal. Both wear the omak, a necklace made of pieces of bamboo, symbolizing the sums conceded to the allies. Each rod indicates that the wearer has given at least eight kina.

PUNAN

Borneo

Feared by other tribes of Borneo who consider them little more than savage beasts, the Punan are proud of their ancient origins, which their legends trace back to the beginning of the world itself. More scientific research has discovered, in the great cave of Niah on the northern coast of Sarawak, vestiges of tombs and dwellings dating from the Paleolithic period of the Stone Age.

The earliest inhabitants of Borneo were Negritos, who were exterminated by the Australian aborigines. They were victims of invaders who came from Malaysia in three successive waves (the Kenyan, Kayan and Iban tribes) and pushed them farther and farther into the interior of the island. The Punan probably descend from these early populations. The first real contact with them dates from 1950.

They are sturdier and more stockily built than other Dayaks (as the non-Muslim groups of Borneo are called, regardless of their tribal origin). In spite of efforts by the Indonesian and Malayan governments to settle them, the Punan lead a seminomadic life, leaving their women, children, the ill and elderly in villages to which they return periodically between migrations through the forest, following an ancestral path of concentric enlarging circles, camping in simple shelters made of branches. Their wanderings, during which they subsist on fruit, berries, and wild game, extend throughout the central plateau of Usun Apau, spreading through the southeast of Sarawak and the central north of Kalimantan.

The Punan are also headhunters. But unlike some other headhunting tribes, they do not massacre wantonly. They cut heads only for ritual reasons, such as to provide magic protection for the clan (in which case the head is rolled in ashes to seal in its vital energy, then hung in the home) or to serve in some important ceremony such as the birth of a chieftain's son or a funeral (in order to facilitate entry into the beyond for the deceased), but especially for weddings.

Their relationship with women is quite extraordinary. Women, they believe, are born without a soul and remain so until they marry. In their soulless state, they are obviously not responsible for errors and sins and thus can lead a totally uninhibited sexual life. But being soulless, they may not engender children. Childbirth in unmarried women is avoided by the common, perfectly acceptable use of various abortive plants. The prospect of marriage brings with it a serious problem. A woman cannot marry until she has found a soul. Her future husband must procure one for her. He sets off on a headhunt. When he returns with his treasure, a lengthy ceremony ensues for the transmission of the soul. It may last three or four days. The medicine man, or shaman, ties the hunted head to the head of the bride and performs a series of complex rites. By interpreting the entrails of sacrificed animals and the flight of birds, he determines whether or not the transmutation has been successful. If not, another head must be sought and the entire ceremony repeated.

Despite their ritual headhunting tradition and the fear they inspire among neighboring tribes, the Punan are not a bloodthirsty people. They live close to nature and feel an integral part of it—the flora as well as the fauna—as their legends attest.

The Broken Pledge

In the beginning there was nothing but sky and water. In the empty immensity of the sky were the sun and the moon, unmoving. Nor was there the slightest movement in the empty immensity of the seas. An eternity passed, then an enormous rock appeared in the sky and fell into the water. When it fell, the sun and moon began to turn. When it hit the water, the water began to move. But the rock was still barren. Another eternity passed. Torrential rains fell, inundating the rock in a veritable deluge. When the rains ceased, mud emerged. From this mud, a myriad of worms came forth and attacked the rock and bored a hole in it.

As the worms bored on, they left behind them debris that stuck to the rock and finally covered it entirely. The debris grew to such a size that the water had to part to make room for it. It was then that Mother Earth emerged. She too, alas, was barren! The sun and moon, which the rock had set in motion, gave birth to the day and night and regulated rainfall. When the sun passed over the earth the first time, it dropped an immense tree trunk which took root. When the moon passed over the earth the first time, it dropped a plant it had nurtured which wound itself around the tree trunk. The tree then acquired its fertile female nature, the plant its fecund male nature. The branches and leaves of the plant covered the tree trunk, and from their union was born a vegetal creature, at the same time male and female. From this came another creature, a hybrid, human and vegetal at the same time, with the torso of a man and vine branches below. This strange legless being was unable to move. A forest spirit divided it into two identical halves and from each half created two beings who were absolutely identical except for one detail: one of them possessed male attributes, the other female, thus removing much of their vegetal heredity. These twins, though still lacking lower members, were able to mate. They gave birth to two children in whom vegetal characteristics were completely absent. They resembled man and woman, except for their missing legs. They managed to move about by rolling over and over . . .

Meanwhile the forest spirits, obeying the Earth Mother, had caused trees and plants to grow. From their bark, they created animals. The two children begged these animals to give them one a buttock, another a leg, another a foot. The animals agreed but on one condition, that the children should never try to kill them once they were able to walk. The children gave their word and the pact was sealed. Now they had legs. They walked, ran and respected their pact with the animals. Their sons did the same, subsisting on fruit and plants. But the following generation began to hunt animals in order to eat meat. The act of slaughter increased with each succeeding generation.

The animals then wished to take back the legs they had lent, considering that their agreement had been broken. The men refused. Friendship gave way to enmity; the animals fled from human beings whose principal activity was now to track them. Thanks to the intervention of the forest spirits, a new pact was made. The men promised to kill only such animals as they needed for their subsistence, and the animals agreed to sacrifice a certain number of victims to the hunters.

Since then, whenever an animal is killed, the Punan beg its soul for pardon, explaining that hunger obliges them to shed its blood. Sometimes, in memory of their vegetal origin, they bury their deceased chieftains in a hollow carved in the trunk of a big tree.

1,2. The territory of the Punan is the central plateau of Usun Apau, stretching from the south of Sarawak, belonging to Malaysia, to the central north of Kalimantan, which is under Indonesian control. Continual rainfall maintains the atmosphere of a hothouse. The dense jungle is furrowed with rivers that are dangerous because of their many whirlpools and violent currents.

1

2

3,4,5. *Alongside the beauty of a luxuriant vegetation (these flowering vines are a hundred feet high), nature has set many traps for men, like scolopendras, a species of poisonous centipede, as well as for animals, such as carnivorous plants.*

3

4

5

1,4,5. The men traditionally wear their hair "bowl-style," with a long ponytail. Their ears are pierced with two holes, the upper one for inserting a warthog tusk (or sometimes tobacco leaves), and the lower for metal hoops.

3. Their earlobes are stretched from infancy by gradually increased weights. The custom explains why the Punan and many of the Dayak peoples are called "long ears."

1

2

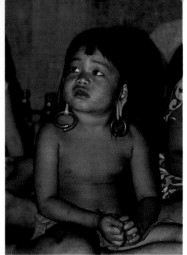

3

4

5

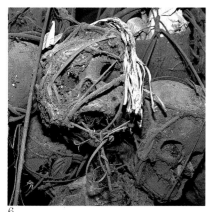

2. *This woman and her young son are perfect examples of Punan physiognomy. The women shave their temples and pluck their eyelashes and eyebrows in order to accentuate the width of the forehead, a sign of beauty and refinement.*

6,7. *Headhunting is a thing of the past, according to the Malaysian and Indonesian governments. But in remote regions of the jungle, human heads still fall. Enemy heads are hung in the huts after being rolled in ashes in order to retain the soul of the dead within the skull. When the Punans' nomadic existence makes it necessary for them to abandon their precarious shelters made of branches, they always take with them these precious trophies, which are believed to protect the home.*

6

7

1,2,3. *Dressed in the traditional loincloth, the Punan hunt with a sarbacane—a blow-gun carved from a hard, heavy wood called casuarina, the only wood able to resist the jungle humidity. Some instinctive sense of ballistics enables them to compensate for the slight natural deformation of the sarbacane (which is about eight feet long) by curving the inside channel just enough to produce a straight trajectory. A metal tip aids balance and permits the sarbacane to be used as a lance for hunting big game. In the bamboo quiver, they carry arrows coated with tadjun,*

3

a poisonous plant. Among the many poisons they concoct, some are meant to kill, others merely to paralyze prey in order to capture it. The principal ingredient is usually an extract from the stone of the strychnos fruit (the source of strychnine).

4. The Punan are usually solitary hunters. But if there is a dearth of food or the prospect of big game, they organize collective expeditions. In this case the elders take the lead, for they are wise in the ways of the jungle, its trails, its secrets and the snares of the "animal master."

4

KOGI

Colombia

Only two thousand Kogi survive in the Sierra Nevada de Santa Marta in Colombia. They are direct descendants of the Tairona, who created one of the oldest and richest civilizations in South America. Little by little, they have been pushed toward the interior valleys, as the provincial government allocates more and more Indian land to white colonists. The Kogi territory is particularly coveted because of its phenomenal vegetation. Banana trees and tropical fruit grow at an altitude of more than eight thousand feet above sea level! This unique situation is certainly due to the fact that these mountain valleys are merely fifty miles away from the warm Caribbean Sea.

The only stone foundations to be excavated in this part of the continent and the most exquisite early examples of the goldsmith's art were discovered in Kogi territory. At the beginning of the sixteenth century these peoples were conquered by the Spanish conquistadors, although they never accepted defeat. The present Colombian government is respectful and rather wary of them, not because of their skills in warfare (which have been completely lost), but because of their fierce pride, which impresses all who come in contact with them.

Even the government officials recognize the Kogi as great lords. They may have lost their material wealth, but they maintain a rich spiritual life. They hold regular assemblies to discuss philosophical and metaphysical problems at great length. They believe that mankind and the entire universe are divided between good and evil, each force being essential to the other. When the perfect balance between them is disrupted, the result is malady, death, and a poor harvest. The same distinction separates men and women. Women personify temptation to beware of, mysterious forces allied to the moon and its cycles; they are respected, but also feared.

The most powerful figure in their legends is a Mother Goddess, rather than an omnipotent god.

The Kogi live in family groups of four or five members in isolated homes in the mountains. For tribal feasts, ceremonies and councils, they gather together in a cluster of mud huts surrounding a ceremonial house or temple dedicated to the Mother Goddess. This temple, a replica of the great universal temple, is crowned by a curious construction shaped like a nest, representing the goddess' sexual organs through whose orifices cosmic forces pass in order to fertilize the sacred earth. A vine rope, symbolizing the umbilical cord, is hung from its topmost point. Through this, the *mamo* is able to communicate with supernatural spirits. The *mamo* is a priest, a healer, the only initiated individual who is learned in the law of the Mother Goddess. He is responsible for "turning the sun around," to regulate the changing seasons.

No tribe is more impressive than the Kogi, for their dignity, and also for their philosophy. When there is perfect equilibrium between good and evil, when neither dominates the other, only then can mankind live in harmony with nature and the universe.

The Law of the Mother Goddess

At the beginning of time, the Mother Goddess created a cosmic egg defined by seven points: the north, the south, the east, the west, the zenith, the nadir, and the center. Inside the egg were nine horizontal layers, each representing a world belonging to one of the original daughters of the Mother Goddess. They differed in color and in fertility. The top layer was white, an arid desert. The second was yellow, composed of sand with a few weeds. The third was ocher-colored, sand with shrubs. The fourth was reddish earth in which fruit-bearing plants grew. The fifth, light brown, was fertile soil, a domain reserved for men. The sixth, dark brown, was land covered with dense vegetation. The seventh, very dark brown, was a lush swamp. The eighth, blackish, was rich sediment. The ninth and last was black, humus of great fertility.

The Mother Goddess had decreed that "all is oneness" and "many must become one." Everything corresponded to everything: the infinitely small was nothing but the replica of the infinitely great, which itself was a reflection of the infinitely small. Thus the mountain peaks resembled the conical roofs of the temples built by men. These sacred sites themselves were created in the image of the great celestial sanctuary, and the tiny underground temples reproduced, on a different scale, the home of the Mother Goddess. At the center of this perfect harmony, the Mother Goddess placed her four original sons at the four cardinal points. The four sons were symbolized by four animals: in the north the marsupial, in the south the puma, in the east the jaguar, in the west the eagle. Hoping to ensure peace to her creation, the Mother Goddess decided to give each of the male animals a complementary female: to the marsupial she gave the armadillo, to the puma the deer, to the jaguar the peccary, to the eagle the serpent. And harmony reigned . . .

Then, unfortunately, came the time of disobedience, of disorder and forgetfulness. The male animals attacked their wives, who from being companions turned into prey. Men acquired vice and sin. War between good and evil raged on earth. The Mother Goddess then ordered the sun to separate the sky into two parts and

the universe into two equal, opposite halves: opposite right was left; opposite light, darkness; opposite heat, cold; opposite the male principle, the female. The first of these (the right, light, heat, and the male principle) belonged to the domain of good, the others to the domain of evil. She decided that from then on, every living thing could develop only if there were a perfect balance between the two opposite but complementary forces. Each of them could exist only in its opposition to the other.

The Mother Goddess instructed her sons to teach humanity the means of achieving and preserving this equilibrium. They came down to earth and created Mount Doanankuivi at the mouth of the Tukurinka River. There they built the first ceremonial house for teaching the Mother's Law. Bunkuase, "the brilliant," the eldest and most perfect of her sons, laid down the strict rules of this law; thanks to his original purity, he knew how to achieve perfect equilibrium. But one of the younger sons, Kashindukua, who had been destined by his mother to cure sickness, was unable to realize this lofty state. He wavered sometimes toward good, sometimes toward evil, and caused Bunkuase much concern. One day he healed men; the next day he taught them incest. Another time, he explained the stars to them, then gave them weapons of war.

Bunkuase nevertheless managed to control his brother's behavior and continued his work of transmitting the Mother's Law to humanity. He waited for a long time in his retreat on Mount Doanankuivi. The first man to feel the divine call in his heart was Bunalyue. He arrived, washed in the waters of the Tukurinka River, and presented himself to Bunkuase. He listened to the Law, received it in his soul, and became the first mamo. Returning to his family, he began to train other mamos, fathers of the fathers of the present mamos. Ever since, the Kogi have heeded the mamo far more than their legal or tribal chieftains, because "he understands the equilibrium" ordained by the Mother Goddess in her Law.

1,2,3. *The Kogi live in the high valleys of the Sierra Nevada of Santa Marta, where the peaks are over 16,000 feet high, yet these valleys are no more than 50 miles from the Caribbean. This double influence creates a unique site: a tropical forest at an altitude of nearly a mile and a half.*

4. *In the center of each village, the temple of the Mother Goddess serves as a ceremonial house as well as a meeting place for men, its access being strictly forbidden to women, who are considered impure. The nest-like construction at the top of the temple (here the*

1

2

temple of Chendukua) represents the female sexual organs, through which heaven descends to fertilize the earth.

5. A mamo (priest-sorcerer) in front of a temple of slightly different architecture. A simple opening at the top of the pyramid roof replaces the usual "nest." Easily recognized by his headdress, the mamo is the spiritual leader of the community. His principal duty is to guide the Kogi, by teaching them the Mother's Law, to yuluka, perfect balance between good and evil.

3

5

4

1,4,5. *The favorite pastime of the men is* poporo: *A hollowed colocynth gourd is filled with shells ground to a powder. The user extracts a small quantity, adds it to* hanyu *leaves (a variety of coca), then chews it tirelessly. The lime of the poporo facilitates the digestion of the highly acid* hanyu. *In time, as the head of the poporo is rubbed by a stick, it gradually acquires a thick coat of hardened*

1

2

3

lime. This custom, with its obviously phallic symbol, is also found among other natives of the Sierra Nevada.

2,3. While their parents work in the fincas, small isolated farms in the mountains, children too young to work remain in the village, looked after by a few older children and adults entrusted with the safeguarding and maintenance of community property.

4

5

1

2

4

In the preparation of panela, a Demerara-type sugar, a press is used to extract sugarcane juice (4) which is then lengthily cooked in fabricas (1). The men take charge of these first two procedures, then the woman's work begins. The liquid thickens as it cools, and is stirred (2) until it becomes a smooth yellowish paste which is then stretched and patiently kneaded (3). Once hardened, the result is panela, an energizing food much appreciated by the Kogi.

On the fincas, men and women work together cultivating cassava (3) and yams (4) in clearings amid banana groves (1). Only women reap the harvest. The Kogi believe there is a mystical relationship between nature, which produces crops, and women, who produce children. The earth is therefore happier when women harvest.

2. The village of Maruamake is a typical Kogi settlement. Small round huts of dried mud are grouped around the ceremonial house, which is higher than the rest. These

villages are deserted while their inhabitants work in the mountains. The village hums with life only during ritual ceremonies or meetings of the clan.

6. All Kogi activities are regulated by a complicated code of rules and taboos. Even the act of building a bridge conforms to strict laws and esoteric rituals concerning the choice of materials, the site and the most favorable time—because bridges, due to their form, belong to the sacred domain of the Mother Goddess.

5. An "abstinent" kuivi: a novice the mamo have chosen to become one of them through magic omens they alone are able to perceive. The kuivi lives a life of strict discipline, temperance, and sexual abstinence with a minimum amount of sleep. When he is deemed ready, the mamo initiates him into the secrets of the Mother's Law.

7. This young man is playing a sacred melody on a "female" flute with five holes. There is also a "male" flute with a single hole.

5

6

7

1

2

3

4

5

1,3,5. After working in the fields, the women prepare meals and look after the children and the home. Furnishing is rudimentary—a few pots and pans, hammocks, perhaps a large stool, replaced only when they are completely worn out. The Kogi diet is based on cassava, yams and plantains.

Women also make the mochillas—small, brightly striped bags in which their husbands carry hanyu *leaves. The Kogi custom is to exchange a handful of leaves whenever*

they greet a friend. It is a matter of prestige to possess a beautiful mochilla.

4,6,7,8. Kogi men are responsible for weaving the coarse fabrics worn by the entire family. They also care for the agave plants and reap the sisal, card it (7), spin it (8), and weave it on looms installed inside the huts. Each person owns a single garment, replacing it when the old one hangs in shreds. The garment of the weaver (6) is no more than eighteen months old.

6

7

8

CHIPAYA

Bolivia

No more than eight hundred Chipaya have managed to survive in Bolivia. They are a strange tribe, detested by the half-bred Bolivians as well as by the neighboring Aymara Indians, who scornfully refer to them as *chullpa* (the name given to the pre-Uros tombs and to the peoples who constructed them), or "the tomb people." "Stupid, dirty, worthless, hopeless, animals" are among the epithets attached to them by their neighbors.

The Chipaya themselves believe they descend from a brilliant empire which was destroyed by the Sun God who was infuriated by their negligence in worshiping him. After a period of chaos and dark, the light finally returned to illuminate a vast salt desert where the Chipaya were born. Many other, less fanciful theories exist. According to the most generally accepted one, the Chipaya are related to the Uros, who disappeared at the beginning of the twentieth century. Spanish historians of the time of the Conquest and later scholars in the nineteenth century were struck by the resemblance of the Chipaya houses to those of the Colla Indians in the southern Andes, and also by the similarity of their customs. Finally, the obvious relationship between the Uro-Chipaya language and that of the Pukina leads one to believe that they descend from southern Colla tribes who became separated from those of the north, possibly due to some lengthy tribal war. None of these theories has been proved, and new ones arise from time to time. An American ethnologist claims to have discovered amazing (and inexplicable) similarities between the Chipaya dialect and the Mayan language of Central America!

The Chipaya are extremely primitive. They believe that magic is everywhere. Their lives are governed by the divinations of initiated tribal sorcerers whose art is handed down from father to son through countless generations. The shaman, or medicine man, can not only predict the future, but can also indicate the most auspicious spot for building a house or select the most favorable name for a newborn child, by interpreting the signs made by coca leaves scattered over a piece of cloth.

Christian missionaries have attempted to convert them. But even those Chipaya who ostensibly accept conversion cling more or less secretly to their ancient gods, and in particular to the Earth Mother. Christian-style tombs are often anointed with the blood of sacrificial goats (blood being the favorite beverage of the gods in the belief of pre-Inca cultures). It is an insurance for protecting the soul in the afterlife. Underneath the Christian crosses in their cemeteries, a little niche is hollowed in which family and friends place food and objects that might be useful to the deceased during his final voyage. Whenever a new home is built, the roof and walls are smeared with fresh blood so that the Earth Mother will favor it with her protection. Under the roof or at the entrance, an Andes wildcat (believed to be inhabited by a good spirit) is hung in order to safeguard the household.

Magic, betrayal, animal friendship, human greed and gratitude . . . these are the themes of their legends, along with the promise of attaining anew the immortality they once possessed but lost.

The Curse

From the heart of Pachamama the Earth Mother, there emerged all sorts of living creatures. Among them was Qamaqe the fox, who was so wily and malicious that men as well as the other animals continually complained about his pranks. One day, however, the men had need for Qamaqe's cunning.

The fertile earth was then well watered and harvests were abundant. The ancient sorcerers took good care of men, who thought it natural to lead a life of ease. Yatiri, the old magician, even wanted to give them immortality. He broached the subject to Pachamama, who accepted on condition that men merit immortality by showing proof of wisdom and foresight. So Yatiri told the men that a stranger would soon visit them. "Receive him," he said, "according to the laws of hospitality, with the warmest welcome. But take care not to be misled by his appearance. Know how to see and judge the person who will come, for he will bear your destiny."

The men paid little heed to Yatiri's warning. Everyone who arrived in the village was lavishly received: cakes, corn and wine were offered generously.

One morning two strangers appeared at the village gate at the same time, an old man and a boy. The old man's wrinkled face was toothless and he carried a shapeless bag. The young boy, on the other hand, had a pleasant face and carried a basket on his arm. When the villagers approached, the old man opened his bag. Inside they discovered to their horror a piece of rotten flesh and three bits of filth: P'usu (pus), Chogo (urine), and Neqe (mud). They thought they were seeing the horror of death. Without even bothering to question the old man, they drove him away with stones. When the young man set down his basket, he smilingly brought forth cakes, which he offered to the villagers. They ate them and rejoiced, convinced that he was the stranger whose visit Yatiri had announced.

When they awoke the next morning after a long night's celebration, both of the strangers had disappeared. Alone in the center of the village, the old sorcerer stood silently weeping. They asked him why he was so sad. With lowered eyes, he replied: "How could you have been so short-sighted? The boy whom you so warmly welcomed was Death itself! And the old man you drove away without even questioning him was bringing you eternal life. Stupid men, you have chased away immortality! Now, not only will you continue to die, but your land will dry up and become barren, and you will know hunger."

In fact, the green earth soon turned into an arid desert covered with salt, and bore no harvest. Still Yatiri, filled with compassion, continued to look after his people. One day he told them there was going to be a great festival in heaven with an abundance of food. It was up to them to find the means of stealing something to eat.

It was then that Qamaqe the fox came on the scene. Driven by his own hunger, he had been prowling around the houses when he heard the old sorcerer's words. He offered his services to the men, assuring them that faithful friends among his animal brethren would help him. Delighted with this stroke of luck, the villagers agreed. Qamaqe ran about the country, asking everyone he met to show him the way to heaven. Neither Asnu the donkey nor Asiro the snake, nor Kusikusi the spider could tell him. K'uti the flea tried to help by taking him on his back and trying to jump as high as the sky, but he was far too small. Finally Qamaqe met Kunturi the condor. Everyone knew that the condor often visited the gods. After much haggling, Kunturi agreed to take the fox to heaven.

The festival of the gods was at its height. As soon as Qamaqe arrived, he forgot his mission and thought only of himself. Like the scoundrel he was, he stole dishes from the kitchen, snatched food from the guests' plates, tried to seduce the women, and went so far as to flirt with Pachamama! Finally, at the end of their patience, the gods tried to chase him away, but thanks to his agility he succeeded in escaping and sought refuge in a granary where he discovered a bag containing delicious little quinoa seeds, food reserved for the gods. He stuffed himself with them to the bursting point.

When he tried to leave the granary, he was spotted by the angry gods. He fled in panic, slipped, dropped down from the top of the sky, and crashed to earth. From his split belly came a spray of quinoa seeds, while his carcass gave birth to a stubborn evil weed.

Ever since, when the Chipaya reap the harvest, they have to separate the quinoa from evil weeds. As they labor, they address Qamaqe: "Father fox, leave these seeds alone. Your lot is well deserved, after your disgraceful behavior on high."

1,2,4. The salar Coïpasa is an immense salt marsh which is a burning desert during the day and so cold at night that it is often covered with a thick sheet of ice. Like the salar of the Uyuni farther south, it hides dangerous pitfalls. Without a perfect knowledge of the "underwater paths," as the Indians say, one risks being suddenly sucked into its depths.

3. *The salar is the principal hunting ground of the Chipaya, where they find duck, Andean geese, and thousands of pink flamingos (unusual at this altitude). To kill the birds, the hunters wield bolas, small lassos made of three strings knotted to form a Y, and weighted at the ends with stones or lead balls.*

2

3

4

1. This shaman, or medicine man, wears pointed earflaps under his hat, the traditional bonnet like that of the young boy in photo 5. The shamans are revered because they can predict the future by studying coca leaves and the entrails of sacrificed animals.

3. Unaccustomed to strangers and shy, these women hide in fear when they see a foreigner approach.

2,4,5. The shape of their houses—earthen "igloos" often covered with a thatched roof—is unlike that of other populations of the high plateaus. Other buildings are identical in

1

2

3

shape, but are smaller and lack the tiny lateral apertures that serve as windows. These are storehouses for quinoa (the local cereal) or rice (imported by truck from Chile). The doors and frame are made of fibrous wood from the giant cactus plants that grow on neighboring mountains.

6. The only irrigation of the Chipaya territory is provided by the Lauca River. Some Chipaya continue to worship it with prayers and offerings, despite the prohibition of this practice by the Bolivian government.

4

5

6

1,3. The Chipaya live in a forgotten region in the province of Carangas, where chullpa are found. Within each of these ancient earthen funeral monuments, mysterious ancestors used to pile their dead, here, near the village of Escara.

1

2

3

4

2,4. Modern cemeteries—Santa Ana de Chipaya, for example—are a perfect illustration of Andean religious syncretism: the coexistence of Christian elements, such as individual tombs crowned with a cross (2), and pagan traditions—skulls often kept separately and anointed with the blood of sacri-

ficed chickens (4), or niches hollowed in funeral mounds for offerings to the departed.
5. One must dig deep in the arid, salty earth to find material suitable for making adobes, sun-dried clay bricks for building houses.

1. Christian missionaries have built a Catholic church and school at Santa Ana, but their influence is superficial. Services are irregular, while the Indians faithfully worship their ancient gods.

1

2

3

4

2. Women weave tunics and ponchos for the men as well as their own dresses from lamb's wool, and especially from llama wool. They spend much time arranging their hair in tiny braids, according to an ancient tradition. Skulls with such braids have been found in the chullpas.

3,4,5. The Chipaya have a distinctive appearance: broad-faced, dark-skinned, slant-eyed, almost Tibetan in aspect, quite different from the neighboring Aymara and Quechua.

6,7. Some activities are communal, such as baking bread and quinoa cakes in the village oven.

5

6

7

KALASH

Pakistan

In three fertile valleys north of Chitral in the Muslim Republic of Pakistan live some 1,300 Kafir (pagans, as the Pakistanis call them)—all that remains of the Indo-European tribes who spoke an Indo-Iranian language and once inhabited the plains of Kabul. The name is derived from "Kafiristan," given to the Afghan side of the Hindu Kush mountain, where the ancestors of the Kalash fled from the plains in order to escape Islamic persecutions during the tenth century. In the nineteenth century the Emir of Kabul ordered their massacre. Only the Kalash, hidden on the eastern slopes, have survived.

The legends of the Kalash attribute their survival, their new homeland, to divine will. Every detail of daily life is governed, they believe, by the will of the Gods as transmitted and interpreted by the *dehar,* a prophet-priest, during his ecstatic trances. The result is a complex code of rules, taboos, and ancient customs. Underlying every act and rite is the distinction between pure and impure, which are antagonistic but complementary.

Kalash women willingly assume their state of inherent impurity. Is it not proven by their menstruation? During this period they are confined in a separate house, the *bashali,* which is also where childbirth takes place. Men are forbidden even to approach it. When repairs are necessary, Muslim workers must be called upon. The *bashali* is generally the most derelict building of the village.

Women are not permitted to enter or approach the sanctuary of a God, nor can they attend ritual sacrifices or take part in one. They are forbidden to eat meat from a male animal, forbidden to milk a cow, for their impurity would be transmitted to it. They cannot enter the barn where cattle and sheep are sheltered. The taboo extends even to the pastures.

The Kalash believe at the same time that rocks and trees are inhabited by good fairies of the female sex. The evil male spirits that roam around them must be placated by various ritual precautions, including sacrifice. Other fairies reign over the springs, forests and herds. Exogamy is obligatory, incest the greatest sin of all. In order to avoid the slightest risk of consaguinity, all members of the clan, whatever their relationship, are considered brothers and sisters. An incestuous act within the clan results in the immediate and irrevocable punishment of banishment from the community. Their strict marriage laws undoubtedly account for the survival of these isolated tribes.

The two most important Kalash festivals take place in the spring and at the time of the winter solstice, during which the spirits of departed ancestors are believed to lend their presence to the festivities. A curious feature of these activities is an oratorical competition among the clans in which the women and girls expound on sexual themes with astonishing audacity, amidst general laughter and ribaldry.

Divine Rivalry

When the prophet Naga Dehar met the god Balumain for the second time, he knew the moment had arrived for the ancient prediction to come true. Many years before, the great god had already appeared to him in the legendary original land of Tysam. He had told the prophet then to lead the Kalash to Bashgal and Waitdesh in order to escape the wave of new religions. Then he had promised to come himself and guide the people to their land of destiny. Naga Dehar had obeyed the will of the god. Now, on this fine autumn day, Balumain, proudly mounted on his horse, returned to see the prophet.

"Wise Naga Dehar, it is time to lead your brothers to the promised land. Your people will settle there forever, to cultivate the fertile land and live in harmony with the spirits inhabiting these sacred places. Go westward. You will come upon three valleys where the Kalash will build their homes. Wait for me there. I will return with other gods."

The prophet again obeyed the divine command. The Kalash settled in the predestined valleys and awaited the arrival of the gods. As promised, Balumain came, accompanied by two other gods, Praba and Mahendeo. The great god summoned the prophet. "Wise Naga Dehar, the supreme creator Kodaï has decided that each of the valleys in which you live should be protected by a god. Praba has already chosen the second valley, but Mahendeo and myself both want the first and we don't know what to do."

Naga Dehar thought for a while, then addressed the gods. "Whichever of you wins the duel shall have the first valley. Listen to me." He described the test. They would have to dig a water canal from the top of the mountain to the bottom of the valley in a single night.

As soon as the sun set behind the mountains, the gods started to work. They worked all night long. At daybreak, only Mahendeo had completed the task. But Balumain refused to accept defeat, claiming that he had to overcome far greater obstacles than his rival. He accused Naga Dehar of favoritism.

The prophet accepted the god's objection and decided that the rivals should face each other in a new duel. He made them climb

to the top of the highest mountain overlooking the disputed valley. It was agreed that the gods should spend the night there. The one who faced the valley when he woke would become its sole and incontestable protector. Another god, Ingao, was to supervise the test. The cold night passed slowly. Agitated by their thoughts, the gods tossed and turned in their sleep. Just before daybreak, Mahendeo was facing south and Balumain was facing toward the valley that was the object of their rivalry. But the god Ingao intervened. He quietly reversed the position of their heads. A few moments later, the first rays of sunshine awakened the gods. Now it was Balumain who faced the Bashgal, and Mehendeo the coveted valley; he had won. Disappointed and angry, vaguely aware that he'd been tricked, Balumain left, determined not to settle in any valley. Only once a year would he visit the Kalash!

Mahendeo went to the first valley, which he shared with Ingao. Praba had long since set his heart on the second. But the third still had no protecting god. Once again Naga Dehar had to intervene. He asked Mahendeo to take charge of the third valley. The god replied that he would give him his decision shortly.

Naga Dehar then went to visit the chieftain of the third valley and handed him a branch of dried juniper and a small stone. "Take this branch, plant it in a hole dug in the ground at the entrance to the village. Sprinkle it with pure water until the hole is full. Take this stone. Wash it and place it next to the branch. If tomorrow morning they have moved, the valley will have a god." And it was done . . . The next morning, the small stone had disappeared and in its place was an enormous rock. The juniper branch had tripled in size and bore magnificent flowers. Mahendeo was willing to be master of the third valley!

This is why the Kalash, who honor all the gods, worship with special reverence Praba in the valley of Birir, Ingao and Mahendeo in the valley of Bumboret, and Mahendeo in the valley of Rumbur. In the first village, they say, can still be found traces of the original divine sanctuary.

1

2

3,4. The houses in the village of Maleidesh (4) are built on the mountain slope. Successive layers of flat stones are laid on planks with mortised corners. Inside, four thick columns support a flat roof consisting of beams covered with slate, branches and earth. The columns often seen over the front door and jutting from the façade (3) are intended for a covered terrace—a project that is rarely completed.

5. A rough, stony road leads from Chitral, the provincial capital, to the Kalash valleys. This access to the outer world might seem beneficial, but it opens a breach in the natural defenses of the "pagan" country. This Kalash and his donkey certainly reach their village more rapidly, but Pakistani merchants and Muslim ulamas (Doctors of Law) also have easier access to it.

1,2. Narrow lanes serve as irrigation canals for the fields below the village, but also hamper the approaches to the homes. The woman and little girl are both wearing a shushut, *the everyday headband that is also the base of the festival headdress* (kupas).

1

2

3. A Kalash at the entrance to the village of Brun (in the valley of Bumboret), standing in front of the gundurik *of his ancestor, a funeral statue representing the deceased in the stylized fashion of divine heroes. It is erected at the same time as the* gandaho, *another funeral statue placed near his home. During festivals, the villagers bring food to the* gundurik *so that the lost ancestor can participate in the feast. They often converse with him.*

3

1,5. Kalash boys and men wear the same bonnet as all the other Afghan and Pakistani mountain peoples. The Kafir Kalash are distinguished from the Muslims by the flowers or leaves stuck in their caps. The bonnets are sometimes embroidered.

4. Acquiring a rifle, even an outdated model, is always an event for these peoples who are surrounded by belligerent tribes (the Pachtous, for example).

1

2

3

4

2,3. *During the initiation that takes place after their first menstruation, young girls decorate their faces with magical motifs, using a dye made from natural pigments. Strictly ritual at first, it has become the customary makeup of young Kalash girls, who are much preoccupied with their appearance and their powers of seduction.*

6. *The* shushut *is a long band that hangs down the back, adorned with beads and cowrie shells. It is worn at the back of the head or, more rarely, on top of it.*

5

6

1. The Kalash dislike cutting trees, which they believe are inhabited by spirits. However, for their personal needs or for the income it provides, they exploit the pine forests, transporting the tree trunks by floating them downriver.

2. In the little town of Grum (in the Rumbur valley) stands the sanctuary of Mahendeo, a god whose cult was probably founded three hundred years ago. Instead of representing the divinity, the artists sculpt a horse's head. Their mounts can be seen, but the gods remain invisible.

1

3. *Women are barred from temples and sacred sites. The* djestak khan *in the village of Brun is the only sanctuary which admits their presence. The entrance is guarded by mythical animals, like the goat heads shown here.*

4. *Women's clothing is adorned with embroidery and jewels symbolizing the sun and stars, in reverence for their divine origin.*

5. *The large woolen headdress women wear during ceremonies is a* kupa. *The abundance of beads, bells, buttons and especially cowries, which bring protection, fecundity and happiness to the woman and her family, are a measure of her husband's wealth. The most elaborate* kupas *are composed of fourteen rows of cowries.*

MURSI

Ethiopia

One of the most original and eccentric branches of the Ethiopian native peoples known as Nara Surma are the Mursi. They are pastoral nomads who raise cattle on the high plateaus bordering the Omo River in the Gemu Gofa region. Their tradition was to leave the Omo Valley during the rainy season beginning in May or June and to move onto the higher plateaus; but since 1982 the drought that has blighted much of Africa has obliged them to remain in the river valley throughout the year.

The origins of these people are unclear, although they are obviously related to the other Omo Valley tribes. They most likely descend from aboriginal populations living farther north, which were driven south into the hills by successive invasions of Nubians and Berber Arabs.

Warriors as well as herdsmen, the Mursi are frequently in conflict with the neighboring Bodi, generally due to a dispute over stolen cattle, violated pasture rights, or in retaliation for an evil spell believed to have been cast over the herd. They are very superstitious. If one asks a Mursi how many head of cattle he possesses, he invariably replies, "More than ten." According to an ancient tribal superstition, knowing the exact number of one's herd brings disaster to it.

The Mursi idea of human beauty—a matter of considerable importance to them—is highly personal. The men are very vain about their appearance, especially their hair. The most prized feature of beauty in their women is also the peculiarity for which the Mursi are most famed, an artificially produced, exaggeratedly protruding lower lip. At the first sign of puberty in a young girl, the long process begins. Two lower teeth are extracted, her lower lip is cut and a wooden plug is inserted in the incision. It is replaced periodically by terra-cotta disks of increasing size. The larger the disk, the more beautiful the young woman, and the higher her marriage price. A great beauty might be worth forty cows.

The origin of this strange custom is unknown, but there are many theories. Could it be an elaboration of the tradition of all Omo peoples who "brand" their women with a cut on the lower lip? (This practice was reported by the first explorers to penetrate their regions in the nineteenth century.) Was it designed to protect the Mursi women from raiding enemy tribes who might abduct and sell them to European slave traders? (A woman thus "mutilated" would have been of little value, thus of little interest.) Or could it be merely a question of aesthetics? The most conservative ethnologists lean toward the theory that the Mursi practice this strange distortion simply because they consider it beautiful. They boast that their women are thus distinguished from the rest of nature: "They do not resemble animals."

Men of the Mursi tribe pass much of their time, when not at war, playing *gadaba*, an ancient pastime known during the reign of King Solomon some 3,000 years ago. It is a simple game of chance. A certain number of seeds are placed in a channel carved in a wooden stick, according to a precise arithmetical system. The first player to use up all his seeds is the winner.

The Four Seeds

"The Great One," father of creation, lived in heaven in perfect harmony with two primordial ancestors. Reflecting the order of the universe, the world of men was also at peace. Men were happy. Unfortunately, a dispute broke out between the sons of the two ancestors and they quarreled over the water, earth, the sun and moon.

Disorder spread throughout the universe. It became so widespread that men lost their lives and nature itself seemed to go mad. Men had hardly sowed the sorgo when torrents of rain flooded the fields and the young plants perished. If the plants survived and matured, they were burned by the violence of the sun as it moved through the sky. The Omo River sank when its water was most needed, and devastated the region when it should have stayed in its course. Men had had enough! They became angry with the sons of the ancestors. The chieftains held a meeting and decided to send an envoy to beg the heavens to calm down. The chosen envoy would have to be the best warrior and be able to undertake a difficult voyage and speak persuasively to the great ancestors. A contest was held among the cleverest, strongest men. The chiefs explained to the winner what was expected of him. They gave him talismans for protection, and sent him forth. The warrior ran for a long, long time. He crossed the plain of tall grasses, the mountain of leafless trees and the river of mud. Then came other plains, other mountains, other rivers. On he ran, heedless to fatigue and injuries. Finally he reached the world of the great ancestors.

He found them calmly seated, watching their sons' quarrel with amusement. The warrior called as witness the Great One, and addressed the great ancestors. Alternating between tears and demands, he warned them that if the disorder continued, men would abandon the earth to settle elsewhere, and the gods would have no one left to worship them and give them offerings. The threat worked. The Great One ordered the sons of the ancestors to make peace, and promised the warrior that order would henceforth

reign throughout the universe. Since the latter seemed doubtful, the Great One said: "The guarantee of our pact will be the regular flooding of the river Omo, a pledge of life and plenty. Take these four seeds. Return to your people and ask them to plant them. May men sow and harvest according to the life of these seeds. There will be four seeds in the sky corresponding to them, which your brothers can see as proof of our convenant."

The warrior held out his hands. As the Great One gave him each seed, he pointed to one of four luminous points that suddenly appeared in the sky, saying, "The first is named Imai. When Imai of the sky grows pale, Imai of the earth will fade and the waters of the Omo will be smooth. The second is named Thaadoi. When Thaadoi disappears from the sky, Thaadoi of the earth will die and the waters of the Omo will rise. The third is named Waar. When Waar of the sky leaves, Waar of the earth will yellow and the waters of the Omo will reach their highest level. The fourth is named Sholbi. When Sholbi of the sky vanishes, Sholbi of the earth will give its flowers to the Omo and its waters will lower."

The warrior placed the four seeds in his bag and returned to his people. He told them of his adventure. They did as he asked and sowed the four seeds. They waited for nightfall and saw the first star appear. Within the time the Great One had promised, the four celestial seeds had appeared one by one, as predicted, and the waters of the Omo followed the predicted rhythm, regulated by the stars. *Bergu*, the regulation of weather, had been given to man. From then on they had different seasons of the year and could anticipate their coming and utilize their knowledge to ensure their sustenance.

Since then, according to the seed of the earth which corresponds to the seed of the sky, the Mursi have known when it is time to sow, cultivate and harvest.

1,2. The muddy waters in the lower reaches of the Omo are infested with giant crocodiles, the largest in the world, sometimes measuring over twenty-five feet long. Customarily herding their flocks onto the high plateaus on both sides of the river, the Mursi have to return to the valley during the dry season. They fear and respect the water spirits and avoid crossing the river in their unstable boats. Some, like this young man (2) dare to do it, but they generally call upon the service of a related tribe, the Batcha, friends of the spirits, to ferry them across.

3. It is impossible (especially for people whose average height is over six feet) to stand erect inside their low or round little huts, made of branches and straw. A family of seven or eight lives in this restricted space, where they still manage to reserve a corner for storing their millet and sorgo.

1,2,3. When they are ready for marriage, around the age of fifteen, the lower lip of young girls is pierced with a piece of flint or wood that has been sharpened and hardened by fire. A sliver of wood is slipped into the hole. When the wound has healed, a terracotta disk is inserted in the incision. Increasingly large and heavy plates are inserted as the lower lip stretches. A sign of beauty and elegance as well as the traditional mark of Mursi women, these plates increase to a diameter of ten inches or more.

1

2

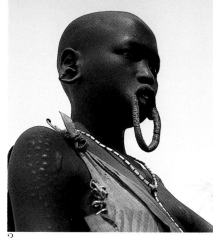

3

4. *Men pluck their eyebrows and shave their entire body and head except for a fine geometric stripe of hair on the crown. They spend hours embellishing themselves and helping one another. Usually unclothed, they sometimes wear a coat made from tree bark that has been softened by pounding it with stones.*

4

1. *This young woman is grinding corn on a millstone. In the receptacle hanging beside her (turned and hollowed by hand, then glazed with clay) she stores the precious salt acquired by bartering with smugglers from Kenya.*

2. *Mursi men do not work in the fields, a task reserved for women. Men guard the flocks and are, above all, warriors. When not hunting game or enemies, they pass their time playing* gadaba, *an ancient game of chance better known under its Arab name of* mangala.

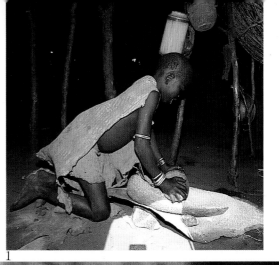

1

2

3,4. *Before attaining womanhood, young girls have to undergo various ritual mutilations. At about the age of ten, the two lower incisors are extracted with the tip of a lance in order to make room for the future plate. During the next two or three years, the ears are pierced for attaching wooden or terra-cotta disks. It is during their fifteenth year that the incision of the lower lip and insertion of the first plate takes place.*

3

4

1,2. Another favorite pastime of the men is improvised dancing, which takes place spontaneously (in contrast to their regular festivals throughout the year). The spectators are very critical, expressing their approval or disapproval by shrill cries and tongue clacking.

The women, clapping and chanting in accompaniment, are dressed in cowhide that is first bleached and then dyed with vegetable tinctures. The brown lines painted on their clothing imitate animal markings (zebra and certain species of antelope).

3. Another ritual scarring of women is done with wood slivers or small pebbles that are inserted under the skin to form traditional patterns. Here, a protective serpent is winding around the woman's body.

3

2

COLORADO

Ecuador

Should the paths of the Colorados happen to cross theirs in the streets of Santo Domingo in northwestern Ecuador, foreign tourists and local citizens alike would stare in wonderment at the sight of the tall, proud natives, their faces painted with wide black horizontal stripes (from the juice of the *huito* fruit), their hair dyed bright red (from extractions of the *achiote,* another tropical fruit abundant in this region). They are members of the Colorado tribe, a branch of the Chibcha, and are descended from some of the most courageous resisters against the Spanish conquistadors. To foreign visitors they are the prototype of primitive tribesmen; to Ecuadorians, they are a sort of "curious animal."

The Spanish invaders gave the Colorados their name, inspired by the red of their dyed hair, which symbolizes courage and virility, and black stripes which evoke the patterns of jungle beasts, certain to strike terror in enemy hearts. Today these decorations are displayed only during tribal festivals or when the Colorados leave their territories to seek provisions in the nearby town.

Unchanged after many Spanish massacres, the survivors continued to resist conquest with legendary valor during the sixteenth and seventeenth centuries. Today they try to defend themselves from the hostility of the white men who covet their lands and whose civilization they reject. Nevertheless, their ancestral traditions are gradually disappearing and their numbers decreasing, for there are only about eight hundred of them left.

The territory of these few remaining Colorados consists of seven separate communities, separated by "civilized" zones. The seven chieftains meet regularly in council houses (from which women are excluded) to make decisions concerning their community life and relations with the Ecuadorian government. The supreme chieftain, the *gobernador,* is accepted as their spokesman by Ecuadorian officials.

Although they have officially converted to Christianity, their traditional belief in supernatural forces and good and evil remains very much alive. These magic forces can be interpreted and manipulated only by their medicine men, sorcerers as well as healers, whose art has been transmitted from father to son for many generations. Spanish historians during the Conquest were in awe with the Colorados' skill in curing ailments and infirmities and chasing away evil spirits. Even today, people come from all over the world to observe their mysterious healing rites and witness their "miraculous" cures—many of which defy all the principles of modern Western medicine.

The medicine men often live outside of the tribal village, apart from the community, in constant contact with the spirits of nature and their ancestors, through whom their secrets are revealed. Their lives are devoted to the practice and transmission of this magic, while the rest of the community frees them from material cares by cultivating their land and providing for their needs.

To the Colorados, sorcery and magic are not only a heritage but a reality, a part of daily life.

The Jealous Sorcerer

When the universe was created, it was made up of three levels. At the bottom was an underground world whose ceiling was our earth. Above it was the earth with its mountains, forests and rivers, just as we know today but without a living creature. At the very top was the upper world with our sky for a floor. Only the upper world was inhabited then. Tall men, larger than we are, lived there. They were skilled hunters, wise and peace-loving.

But there was no cosmic order. The stars collided, the planets strayed, the sun and moon, in love with each other, were inseparable; and all this worried the big men.

An old shaman decided to create gods to govern the universe. With magical gestures, it was done. The gods were born and imposed their laws. Soon order and regularity appeared. The sun and moon lived apart; day followed night, which was followed by another day. The stars formed set patterns in the sky and everything turned in the same direction. Beyond this well-ordered universe, high above, there was another sun, larger and more brilliant, perfectly immobile, which not only governed the laws of creation but was their eternal guarantee. Then a new god, Taïta Dios, appeared. He pulled himself up to the great immobile sun, merged with it, and became the only god. His first words were: "I am the beginning and the end of everything. I am one and you must obey my rule." First the big men, then all the gods and goddesses rallied to him. Only "the old woman," the most ancient divinity, decided to pretend to obey, secretly vowing to destroy the power of the new master. She used thousands of tricks and set a thousand traps, but the supreme god magically escaped her treachery. Realizing that she could not harm the Only One, she then decided to attack his creation. She had noticed that the heavenly water did not appreciate the new authority which obliged it to conform to a regular cycle and a precise path. The old woman visited the water several times, first with little gifts and words of consolation and then with offerings and words of incitement to rebel.

One day the old woman made the water drink a magic potion designed to weaken her spirit. She then was able to persuade the

water to flood the world. Celestial floods crashed down upon the big men when Taïta Dios was asleep. Their cries of despair reached him too late for him to help. However, he managed to save a few of them from the disaster and kept them close to him.

From them and in their image, he created a new race of men that he placed in a second world, the one which is ours. Humanity was born; but it was smaller in stature and far less wise than the big men. The old woman, who had not yet satisfied her hatred, then descended to earth and entered the lower world. In the subterranean shadows, she met the devil, a former servant of Taïta Dios who had been exiled for betraying the supreme master. He had created a race of dwarfs who served him faithfully and whose movements caused the earth to quake. The old woman formed a pact with him. Then they summoned the water, her former accomplice.

Taïta Dios had forbidden the water to crash down from the sky, threatening to freeze it forever if it did so. It was to produce only regular rainfall; this caused the water great resentment. The three conspirators decided to create whirlpools. When this was done, they hid them at the bottom of the rivers. Next, they persuaded magic female beings of great beauty, with fair hair and eyes, to lure men to the fatal whirlpools. Their terrible plot escaped the vigilance of Taïta Dios, and many men were drowned.

Since then, Colorado mothers advise their children to run away from any apparitions near the water, for if a sailor is bewitched by the infernal creature and steers his boat toward a whirlpool, the devil, with a fiendish laugh, will drag him to the bottom of the river.

1

1,2. The Colorado territory is much smaller than it once was and today is restricted to a reservation bounded more or less by the Babahoyo, Chihuipe, Poste and Tahuazo rivers. The frequent rains and a sultry climate have created a thick forest streaked with numerous waterways. In this area, a canoe is often the only practical form of transportation.

3. While a few of the larger villages are situated near road junctions, most of the houses are scattered in clearings far from the fields, so that the noise of their work will not disturb the spirits who protect their homes.

3

1. The everyday dress of Colorado women is only a striped cotton skirt. This one is wearing the more formal coat and scarf reserved for festivals or going to market in Santo Domingo. Albinos, such as the woman in the foreground, are not uncommon in this ethnic group.

2. Tradition persists among these Indians. Although long converted to Christianity, they still maintain many of their beliefs and rites and respect the counsel of elders like this old clan chieftain.

1

2

3

3,5. *Their houses are usually built on piles to isolate them from the ground and to provide shelter for their pigs and chickens under the house. Often consisting of no more than a floor and a roof, they are divided into two sections: one for cooking, the other for sleeping.*

4. *An ingenious cradle rocked by a system of strings. The straw matting protects the baby from animals and insects on the ground.*

4

5

1,2,3,4. The Spanish conquistadors were so impressed by these people's unusual hair style that they gave them the name of colorados ("reddish"). The men shave their heads except for a long fringe at the top. By grinding seeds of the achiote *fruit they create a sticky red dye which is insoluble in water. They fashion this mixture into a veritable helmet that remains intact for about a week be*fore starting to crack. The entire operation is then repeated. Meanwhile it withstands bathing and work. At puberty, the young boys' nostrils are pierced and a piece of chonta wood is inserted in the hole. The boy is then considered a man, entitled to use achiote. Another custom is to draw black lines on the face and body with huito *juice (another tropical fruit).*

1

2

3

4

5

The community theoretically obeys a single chieftain, the gobernador; but the shaman's occult authority is, in fact, greater. The present gobernador, Nicanor Calazacon (4), fills both roles. The shaman utilizes natural elements such as rainwater collected in sacred gourds (7) and animals or serpents (5), to concoct miraculous ointments. The fame of Colorado healers has spread far beyond the national boundaries. Fernando, a healer (6), is shown here seated on his porch. In front of him, suspended from the roof, are two marimbas (ritual xylophones) on which his assistants play while he prepares his magic potions in the secret recesses of his home.

6

7

ASMAT

Irian Jaya, New Guinea

The environment in which the Asmat live is so hostile—composed, as it is, of swamps, quagmires, dangerous animals and enemy tribes—that these descendants of Paleolithic Negroid strains which settled in New Guinea are perpetually concerned with survival. They spend their time trying to strengthen the bonds between their various clans and between the living and their dead ancestors by means of traditional rites.

The *bisj*, a totem pole or column of ancestors, is carved from the trunk of a mangrove or sago tree, both of which are sacred and magical. It is, of course, a phallic symbol, but it is also a means of associating the departed ancestors with the daily life of the community. It is placed in the *yeu*, the ceremonial house.

The *papisj* is a marital exchange between two couples. The men agree on the conditions; their wives must be consulted, however, and must consent. On rare occasions, there are also community *papisj*, involving all of the clans of the village. Some ethnologists view this practice as a means of seeking revenge on an unfriendly environment or of exorcising misfortune and death. It is as if man, by an excessive display of sexuality, could compensate for the high death rate by creating mass births. The *papisj* is by no means an orgy. It is, on the contrary, a solemn rite with stringent rules. Adultery is severely prohibited and is punished by exile from the clan and therefore from the village. In this perilous territory, it is the equivalent of being condemned to death.

Adoption is the third rite of special significance to the Asmat. It may be a private matter. A particular family may simply wish to adopt a new member. Or it may be a public adoption, in which case the entire village adopts several men and women. The women stand in a row, one behind another, their legs spread to form a passage (symbolizing the vagina) through which the adopted persons crawl, emerging at the end to start a new life. Tribal adoption is a means of broadening the network of friendly alliances and of increasing—thus strengthening—the clan.

The site of these and other Asmat ceremonies, such as initiation and marriage, is the *yeu*, where the Asmat also frequently go to consult and converse with their ancestors. Because of the severity of the climate, the *yeu* must be rebuilt every four or five years. Once the new structure has been completed, each man of the tribe puts some insect larvae in the trunk of a hollowed sago tree, which is placed in the center of the sacred area. The women then dance around it. Then the trunk is split and the larvae escape. It is a fertility symbol of new life.

Headhunting is still practiced by the Asmat, despite assertions to the contrary by the Indonesian government. It is related to their fertility and initiation rites. The practice is also a means of providing magical protection, since vital energy is believed to be concentrated in the head, particularly in the brain. The brains of enemy heads are extracted and eaten. Even then, they believe, the head retains vitality, so the lower jaw must be removed to prevent it from biting its foe. The Asmat carefully save the skulls of friends and use them as headrests. They feel these offer protection when they sleep at night, and call them "fathers."

The Man Who Was Bored

War, a sea hawk, was flying across the distant western waters when he was alerted by the cries of birds who had spotted a corpse floating on the Sea of Arafura. Struck by the beauty of its skin, the birds did not dare to touch it. War circled overhead three times, then landed on the corpse and studied it carefully. He too was impressed by its perfection. Such a creature could not die! He breathed into its nostrils to revive it. As War flew away, the drowned man's eyes opened and the breath of life filled his lungs. He swam to the nearest shore, the muddy bank of the Cenderawasih. There he sat down, and he remembered that his name was Fumeripitsj, "the wind man." In a previous existence he had seduced his brother's wife and been forced to flee from his village. During his flight, his canoe capsized and he drowned. The current had then swept his body to the open sea, where he had drifted until War discovered him.

The memory of his sad fate caused him to weep and weep. He swore never again to commit such a sin. When his tears had ceased, he looked around. There was not a soul in sight and he felt terribly lonely. He explored the riverbank, searched the forest far and wide, and was forced to face the fact that he was alone . . . and he was bored. A few days later, he cut some tree trunks and built the first *yeu*, the house of spirits. He sat inside and waited. Nothing happened. He was still all alone, and he was bored. He decided to carve two statues in his own image, one a man, the other a woman. When they were finished, he placed them inside the *yeu* and spoke to them, hoping for a response of some kind, but nothing happened. He was alone . . . and he was bored. Then he called upon the wind and asked it to help him. The south wind answered his appeal: "Go into the depths of the jungle. Look for a 'tree woman' in the image of a human being. When a bird comes and eats her head, chop the tree down and carve a *tifa* from its trunk. Then wait for the first rain. When it falls, play the magic drum and you will see the statue come to life to keep you company."

Fumeripitsj went into the jungle. He walked all day and night. In the morning, he came upon a sago tree and understood at once

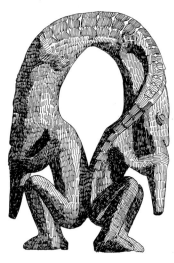

what the wind had told him. The tree's roots were like human feet, the trunk was like the body, the branches like arms. In the center of the crown of leaves around the top was a huge fruit like a human head. Just then a calao arrived and began to eat the fruit. Yes, this must be the tree woman! Fumeripitsj chopped down the tree and took the trunk into the *yeu*. He carved from it a magnificent *tifa*. Then he began to play with it. The two statues came to life and began to dance a jerky dance. At last Fumeripitsj was happy. He was no longer alone, no longer bored.

Every day he played on the magic drum and delighted at the sight of the living statues. Unfortunately, one day an enormous black crocodile came out of the river when Fumeripitsj was not there. The monster rushed to the *yeu* and smashed it, then decided to attack the statues. Dashing back as fast as his legs could carry him, "the wind man" fell upon the crocodile. A terrible fight ensued, lasting for many moons. Fumeripitsj was finally the victor. He killed the crocodile and cut its corpse into three pieces with a sharpened stone. Mad with rage, he flung the first piece so far that it lost its color; when it fell beyond the seas, it gave birth to the white race. His anger was slightly appeased when he threw away the second piece, which landed less far away and lost only part of its color. It was brown when it landed in the middle of the sea, and was the origin of the dark race. By the time "the wind man" grasped the third piece, all his anger had vanished. With a disdainful gesture he dropped it on the ground, and from it originated the black race, that of the Papous.

Then he summoned War. He entrusted him with the safeguarding of the two statues. The sea hawk carried them far away into the west, to the *Safan,* land of happiness and abundance. From there they could continue to watch over their descendants, the Asmat.

In memory of these events, the Asmat tribe imitate the jerky movements of their wooden ancestors when they dance and as they chant the name of Fumeripitsj.

1. These boatmen are about to drag a heavy canoe (hollowed by fire and ax out of a tree trunk) over several hundred meters in order to bypass the lengthy meanderings of the river Kronkel.

2. Asmat sculptors are renowned. This one is carving a stylized human effigy in the prow of a boat, symbolic of vanquished enemies, who are tied to the prow to be carried off as captives. His tools are fire-hardened sticks of wood and blades made from sharpened seashells.

1

2

3

4

5

6

3,6. Asmat villages are usually small (two or three hundred inhabitants), and consist of large huts grouped side by side in two straight lines on either side of a central lane. The huts are built on stilts for security and because of the frequent floods.

4,5,7. The Asmat believe in reincarnation. They think every birth is the result of the impregnation of the mother by the spirit of an ancestor of the same sex as the baby. Since masculine and feminine domains are separate and distinct, women raise the daughters, while the men take charge of the boys as soon as they are weaned, at four or five.

7

1,2,3,4,5. *For every important occasion in their lives, during ceremonies and in war-time, the Asmat decorate themselves: first with paint—predominantly white, obtained from sago flour or the lime from burnt sea-shells; then with feathers on their heads—the multicolored plumage of birds of paradise, the white of cockatoos, the tapered black feathers of the cassowary; and finally with nasal ornaments, most often the* bipane (2), *cut from a large white shell in the shape of boar tusks. The* bipane *is a symbol of valor and strength, both of which virtues the bearer acquires by inserting it in the nasal mem-*

brane that is pierced at puberty. The women also wear feathers, but never paint their faces.

6. Precious skins of the kuskus *(a small marsupial) are used to make the bands of the headdresses decorated with shells. The cutouts on the wooden shield are a stylized version of the* bipane. *Enforcing the shield's symbolic strength is the ancestor figure carved on top, who offers magic protection. In addition to white, black paint (soot mixed with earth), and red dye (from berries or baked clay) are used in decorating their bodies and faces.*

1. *The most prestigious nasal ornament is the* otsj, *carved from a pig bone—and sometimes from a human one, which enhances its value. The one worn by this Asmat was, he claims, cut from the tibia of an enemy whose head he also preserved. The black paint around his eyes is a sign of participation in a war raid.*

2,3. *This is a collective adoption ceremony. Around a group of* tifa *players (ritual drums), the future adoptees, entirely painted in white, and their designated fathers, who have adorned them and given them weapons, dance in preparation for their meeting with the deceased ancestors. During the final phase of the ritual, the adoptive mothers will breast-feed their new children. From then on, the latter will be part of the community.*

2

1

3

AKHA

Thailand – Burma – Laos

Unrespected and unloved by the other tribes of the Thailand mountains, disdained by the Burmese and Thai population, the Akha are disapproved of for being primitive, violent, ignorant and dirty. Yet they are merely simple mountain people who wish above all to preserve their independence. Unfortunately, their stubborn and excessive practice of burning their farmland, destroying roots and stumps before planting anew, has gradually impoverished their territory and ruined their environment. This practice is one of the principal causes of the decline and the inevitable extinction, sooner or later, of the Akha. A sad ending for a tribe that has survived many centuries of migration and persecution.

Their distant ancestry is related to the Lolo or Yi who inhabited the highlands of eastern Tibet until the beginning of the present era. During the second century B.C., a portion of this population, having for some mysterious reason gradually lost its resistance to the intense cold of those regions, descended into the valleys and followed the rivers southward. One branch forged farther than the others; an important part of it settled in the Yunnan province of China in the seventh century A.D. They were the Akha. But they had not yet reached the end of their migration. Persecuted by their neighbors during the nineteenth century, most of them set forth again toward the south and established settlements in Burma and northern Thailand at the beginning of the twentieth century. Today some 30,000 Akha live in Thailand, some 2,000 in Laos, some 5,000 in Burma and many more in China, where their exact number has not been divulged by the government.

The community is ruled with extraordinary precision, considering their reputation as uncivilized primitives. Every detail of daily life is regulated by the rites of *akhazang,* "the Akha way." The rites are a vast collection of traditions, epic and poetic tales, mythology, moral precepts, social laws and conventions to which all members of the tribe are obliged to conform. The individual responsible for administering and transmitting this heritage is the *pima.* He is aided in his task by supernatural forces with which he is in contact. Two other persons are important in Akha society: the *dzoema,* who represents moral and legal authority and supervises the welfare of the community, and the *buseh,* who assists and, if need be, replaces the *dzoema* as well as dealing with the Thai administration.

According to Akha tradition, the entire world is divided into two opposite but complementary halves, male and female. Each one has its duties, its rights and rituals. Villages, forests and the trails within them are masculine; houses and farmland belong to the feminine domain.

Akha women are unusually hard-working. Proud of their diligence, they scornfully compare it to the idleness of their menfolk, most of whom are opium addicts. Their cultivation of the opium poppy is not entirely for its interest as a euphoria-inducing drug. It also plays an important role in the medical and mystical traditions of the Akha.

When A-poe-mi-yeh Had Enough

Long ago, the spirits and men lived in the same world, a world created by A-poe-mi-yeh, the great ancestor. They shared the same houses and the same food. But they quarreled continually, mainly over matters of theft.

The spirits and men alike were thievish. The spirits slept during the daytime and the men at night, and each robbed the other during their sleep. At sunrise, the men would shout that the spirits had robbed them; at sunset, the spirits would make the same complaint about the men. Their bickering day and night prevented A-poe-mi-yeh from getting any rest. The disputes became so noisy that the great ancestor, tired and exasperated, decided to make them live apart. He created two completely different worlds, one on high and the other below. Spirits and men had only to decide where they wished to live.

When the hour of choice arrived, it was daytime. The men were wide awake and thus had first choice. They chose the world below, which was full of fruit and game. So they descended to earth and settled there. When the spirits awoke, they were very annoyed when they learned that they would have to be satisfied with the world on high, which was airy and humid. They simmered with rage for a long time before they thought of their best means of revenge—water! Water was the only communication between the two separate worlds. It fell from the sky to water the earth and swell the rivers. They enticed it with consoling words and numerous gifts and persuaded it to take them to earth. The water accepted, but only during half of the year, when its rainfall was heaviest; for in the middle of the torrents nobody would be able to detect the spirits hidden there.

So the spirits descended to earth, concealed in the water. Suddenly sickness, plague and violent death appeared. The men rushed in panic to A-poe-mi-yeh in his heavenly abode. After listening to them, he ordered them to build gates to protect the entrances to all the villages before the rains came, and to attach masks to them representing rapacious birds with sharp beaks and

snarling dogs with bared teeth. They should also place magic statues, male and female, on each side of the gate. This would protect the villages from the spirits. The men on earth did as A-poe-mi-yeh advised. Their misfortunes then ceased. The frightened spirits no longer dared approach the villages, but they had not given up. In the meantime, the men gradually forgot the danger.

Time passed. Whenever a problem arose the men would consult A-poe-mi-yeh, sometimes bothering him with trivialities, and the great ancestor became increasingly annoyed. One day a man wished to live one hundred years. How could he solve the problem of old age and death? They decided to ask the great ancestor. He said nothing. They again explained the purpose of their visit, repeated their questions and still received no answer. They beseeched him a third time.

It was then that A-poe-mi-yeh thundered, "You keep on bothering me. You continually trouble my rest and disturb my meditation. I've had enough! From now on, during every rainy season, the spirits will try to catch you whenever you are careless or negligent. Even if you manage to ward off their assaults, none of you will ever live one hundred years!"

Since then, it's true that the evil spirits sometimes succeed in getting past the gates to bring misfortune to the villages. And never has an Akhan lived as long as one hundred years!

1. The tragedy of the Akha people is continued here. Observing ancestral traditions and ignoring official warnings, they still burn their fields after the harvest, thus impoverishing the soil, destroying the forests and drying up the springs.

3. Fields where rice and vegetables are grown are left fallow periodically and serve as pasture for buffalo.

2,5. For reasons of security, the villages are built high up on the mountains but below the crest, which is the abode of spirits. The invisible line separating masculine and feminine domains extends to the interior of their homes. There is a partition dividing them into two sections, one for men, the other for women, with a space reserved for sheltering their pigs at night.

4. The gates and statues at the entrance to each village are magic portals barring access by evil spirits bearing malady and death.

2,3,4,5,6,7. *The feminine headdress,* u-coe, *which can weigh as much as eleven pounds, varies from one village to another but its principle remains the same. First is a cotton bonnet on which little girls hang their first beads and silver balls and over which women attach a light bamboo frame. That is progressively adorned with a multitude of decorations: coins, balls, strands of wool and vari-colored feathers. The most famous* u-coe *are those of the Thai from Napey (3,4) and the Burmese from Loi Mwe (2,7).*

2

3

5

6

4

7

113

1. The men's headdress, worn mainly by the Akha of Burma, probably derives from a Chinese or Mongol tradition. The bracelets of plaited fiber the man is wearing on his right wrist protect him from evil spirits.

2. Supported by a bamboo pole, this woman from the Keng-Tung region in Burma operates a wooden carding comb with her hands and two bamboo pedals with her feet.

Cotton weaving is the exclusive domain of Akha women, and their greatest pride. Their skill is probably due to the fact that their ancestors lived for centuries in Burma and southern China, in contact with past masters in the art of growing and weaving cotton.

3. Smoking his long opium pipe, this man is plaiting strips of split bamboo to make an inner partition for his home.

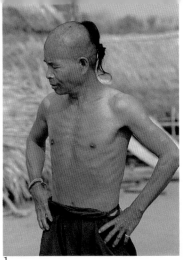

1

2

3

4,5. On their way to the fields, women cover their headdress (often finely embroidered) with a scarf. They hardly ever remove the u-coe, not even during the night. Only when it might be damaged is it removed. They carry heavy burdens in the ancient manner, with the weight divided between the forehead and back, and the back relieved by a supporting plank.

4

5

CUNA

Panama

A group of little islands in the Western Caribbean form the archipelago of San Blas. In some of these idyllic miniature Gardens of Eden, and on the nearby shores of the Panama peninsula, dwell 18,000 members of a peaceful, happy tribe, the Cuna. This, at least, is the name by which they are known to strangers.

Most of the Cuna live on the islands, and most of them are fishermen. Others live in isolated villages on the mainland coast or farther inland. They raise corn, sugarcane, sweet potatoes, plantains, fruit trees and, above all, coconuts, their principal source of revenue.

The manner and means of their settling in this earthly paradise are shrouded in mystery and difficult to determine. Their own version is woven with many legends, mingled with a few strands of historical fact. It seems most likely that they descend from the Cueva Indians of Colombia, who fought against the Spanish conquistadors in the sixteenth century. Driven north by native warrior tribes, they probably made their way into the region of the Gulf of Uraba (where some of them still reside) during the seventeenth or eighteenth century. By the nineteenth century most of them had migrated to the San Blas archipelago, where they settled permanently and are found today.

Belief in a supreme god supported and surrounded by a host of magic spirits holds an important place in their life. Clinging to their ancestral legends, they have withstood all efforts to convert them to Christianity. The spirits, they believe, live in the *kalu* (celestial dwellings inaccessible to human beings). A perpetual war is waged between the spirits benevolent toward the Cuna and those which wish them ill. The latter send sickness and death, and attempt to rob them of their *purba*—a unique conception that might be best described as a guardian angel "which is within us and protects us." Their religious life involves various ceremonies presided over by tribal priests, the *nele,* who alone are able to communicate directly with the spirit world. The *nele* are endowed with many other powers. They exorcise evil spirits with the use of magic statues and secret rites and, most important, they are able to restore the *purba* to those who have been robbed of them. The Cuna also believe that when they die they will go to a paradise where they will find everything they have ever known or possessed on earth—but this time all will be in solid gold! They do not doubt for a minute the veracity and validity of their traditional beliefs. They willingly accept the benefits of modern civilization, but refuse concepts foreign to their mentality. A typical example was that when the governor of Panama ordered a telephone system installed on some of the islands, the Cuna believed the wires were magic cords permitting God himself to communicate with their tribal chieftains.

Their happy, peaceful existence is increasingly menaced by the population explosion of the blacks. Even more, perhaps, is the Pan-American highway project, which would cut right through the center of the Cuna territory and undoubtedly destroy their paradise on earth.

The Fire Thief

Water and earth had long existed before God gave fire to our world. Only one being possessed it then, El Tigre. Why and how he acquired it is a mystery, but he alone kept warm and ate cooked meat. All other living creatures, men and animals alike, shivered from the cold and had to be satisfied with raw meat. The situation got worse when the sluice gates in the sky opened during the rainy season, and even worse at night, when Olonitalipipilele, the moon star, appeared. The moon, accompanied by his six sons, was imprisoned on high in punishment for the crime of incest. Seeing what was happening below, he was upset.

He sent his eldest son, Udole, to help the suffering humans on earth. Udole went to see their priest, the *nele*, and explained that their condition would improve if they had fire. They would have to acquire it from El Tigre. The *nele* assembled the men and animals and told them of the word from heaven. Together, they decided to find El Tigre and ask him for fire. When they approached the feline's home, the rainy season was at its height. A swollen river separated them from the other bank on which El Tigre lived, so they sent Guacamayo, the macaw with the silver tongue, to negotiate with the wild beast.

It was very cold and El Tigre had set his fire pot underneath his hammock. The macaw fluttered around him and he woke up in a very bad humor. He tried to catch the bird, then realizing that it was hopeless, he lay down and said, "Brother bird, why have you come to disturb my sleep? It could cost you your life." "Brother tiger, I have come in the name of all creatures who walk, fly and swim, to ask you for fire. We are cold out there and can eat only uncooked meat."

El Tigre pretended to think for a long time. Suddenly he pounced on the hapless unsuspecting Guacamayo and gobbled him up. Then he went back to sleep. Everyone on the opposite riverbank had witnessed the drama. They decided to try force next time. They sent the strong and valiant peccary, but he too was killed by El Tigre. The dismayed men and animals didn't know what to do next. Then the iguana, renowned for his clever ways, offered his help. They accepted with enthusiasm.

He crossed the river and found El Tigre, who eyed him closely.

"Brother iguana," he said, "what are you doing here? It could cost you your life."

"Brother tiger, you would be terribly mistaken to kill me. I can be useful to you. I've noticed that every night while you sleep, the fire dies down and often you save it only by waking up in time. You cannot keep your eyes open indefinitely. I propose a bargain: I will watch over the fire while you sleep, and rest while you are awake. Thus the fire will be constantly watched over and both of us will be warm and eat cooked meat. After all, why should I care about the lot of other creatures?"

"Brother iguana, you have convinced me. I accept your offer. But if you have tricked me, I will kill you." The bargain was sealed. The two confederates started a new life, watching over the fire in turn. This lasted during two moons. Each evening the tiger confidently fell into a deep sleep. One night the iguana set his plan in action. He stuck a few burning embers in his spiny back, urinated on the fire, dashed to the river, and swam across it. The embers were still burning when he reached the other bank. But the iguana refused to give them to the men and animals who were waiting so impatiently. Furious, they jumped on him. He dropped the embers and saved his life only by escaping into the forest.

In the meantime, El Tigre was awakened by the cold. He saw the extinguished fire and understood that he had been tricked. He saw the men and animals across the river warming themselves at a blazing fire, eating roasted meat and singing. El Tigre screamed in rage to the star of the night: "Olonitalipipilele, treacherous moon, you have helped your sons, the men and animals, steal my fire. You have condemned me to be cold and eat raw meat! So be it! Night and day I will prowl about and kill every living soul I find!" The moon trembled and tried to warn the living creatures of the danger. But they were too happy to hear him, and El Tigre set forth on his relentless pursuit . . .

That is why, ever since, the iguana hides in trees and why the tiger is the deadliest enemy of man.

1,3. An archipelago of islands in the Caribbean and the neighboring Panama coast form the Territory of San Blas. On these tiny islets, the houses are usually clustered around a central square where the council house—villages of Mulatupu (1) and Ustupu—is located. (The suffix "tupu" means "village.") Sometimes they are grouped around the home of the sahila *(traditional chieftain) or the* kantule *(master of rites).*

2. On the coast where space is no problem, the villages spread into the seaside palm groves, like this one near Punta Escoces.

1,2,3,4. *The Cuna sail between the islands and the coast in* cayucos, *canoes carved from the trunks of coconut trees. From infancy they learn to interpret "the color of the waves, the word of the wind, the paths of the sea, which is the land God gave to the Cuna," an old Indian saying. The Territory of San Blas became the collective property of this ethnic group after the Indian revolt of 1925. Irritated by the continual intervention of the Panama government, the Cuna proclaimed the Republic of the Tule. The government was able to quell the rebellion only by permitting the Cuna to live in total autonomy.*

1

2

3

4

5

5. *Fishing is men's work. At sea they use nets, but they prefer to fish in the muddy yellow waters along the coast, where fish are abundant. They wield two-pointed harpoons with consummate skill.*

1,3. Women wear a small gold ring in their nose, paint their face red with the tropical fruit *achiote, and* draw a line down the bridge of the nose with the black juice of the huito *fruit. They wrap their arms and lower legs in* canilleras, *strings of colorful beads wound around their calves.*

2. *The central hearth of the home is sacred. Its precise location is designated by the* nele (priest), *thus is known to the gods. Situated in the exact center of the house, it is never displaced.*

124

4. *The principal source of income for the Cuna is the coconut, even though Panamanian traders have been lowering its price in recent years.*

1,2,3. *Young Cuna women are preoccupied with their appearance and especially their attire, and spend much of their time fashioning their basic garment, the* mola. *It is a square piece of material made by assembling scraps of fabric sewn one on top of another. The successive layers form rich patterns of birds, flowers and real or mythical animals. It is never embroidered. Two* molas *are required to make a shirt—one for the front, the other for the back. Older women sometimes repeat the pattern of the neckline at the bottom of the skirt. This tradition is said to date from the time the Cuna "dressed" their nude bodies by painting them in bright colors.*

1

4. *Women hold an important place in Cuna society. They possess ritual and family authority. After their first menstrual periods, young girls are isolated in* surba, *houses of initiation of females, from which men are strictly barred. After rites during which they drink* inna, *the sacred potion of the initiated, they are considered women. Until their recognized womanhood, girls are not permitted to paint their faces.*

3

4

DOGON
Mali

"Many moons ago, our ancestors drove the little red men from the mountain." Thus the Dogon explain their present settlement on the rocky slopes of the cliff of Bandiagara in southern Mali, an imposing barrier almost 650 feet high that stretches for twenty-five miles to the frontier of Mali and of Burkina Faso. The caves of their predecessors, the Tellem ("the discovered people" to the Dogon), can still be visited.

It seems most likely that the Dogon tribe descended from the great Mande empire of pre-Islamic times. After their golden age in the thirteenth and fourteenth centuries, this powerful empire disintegrated in the face of persistent attacks by nomadic warriors during the fifteenth century. Driven toward the northeast, the Dogon ancestors were halted in their migration by the formidable Bandiagara cliff. They chased the Tellem from their caves and at first inhabited them themselves. They then built their own homes on the summit and shelves of the cliff. Never have they established villages on the plain, which has been reserved for farming. Every inch of arable land is treasured.

Within the rigid caste system devised by the Dogon, the noblest social class is agricultural, the lowest is that of blacksmiths. Male children of the higher classes are circumcised and female children are excised. These are marks of their social superiority, forbidden to children of lesser birth. However, it is deceptive to apply our sophisticated ideas of "upper" and "lower" classes to these simple people. The status of the smiths, for example, although the lowest caste of all and therefore disdained, is at the same time respected for its heritage of healing powers. They are believed to be in contact with supernatural forces.

It is forbidden to marry outside of one's caste. The council of elders as well as the family patriarchs see to it that tribal tradition is respected in every detail of its strict morality.

Within the family, man is the absolute master. Only the male head of the family is entitled to own land and to possess the key to the granary. His word is law and must be obeyed. It is he who presides over the family altar and performs sacrificial rites in honor of the ancestors, of God, of the spirits in water, trees and stones, which are all considered children of God.

Before a young man can marry and form a family of his own, he must have produced three or four children by the same woman, while living with other unmarried men in a hut near to the paternal home. When a couple is at last permitted to wed, they settle in a home of their own close to the patriarchal house and cultivate the father's land.

Family solidarity is of great importance to the Dogon, who measure a man's riches according to the size of his family and the number of his friends. It is therefore not surprising—although curious—that one of their ancient legends should reflect a regret for having lost the gift of engendering twins—certainly the most rapid means of increasing the size of a family clan.

The Pale Fox

Amma, the first and foremost god, held a ball of clay in his hand. He tossed it into the air, causing it to spin. It spun faster and faster, like a whirlwind so violent that the ball burst, forming the egg of the world. This egg was divided into two parts. In each there was a pair of twins, and each pair consisted of a male and a female. Before the egg had time to hatch, one of the males escaped. He wanted to be the first to take possession of the universe. His name was Ogo.

He fell into the vast void of the non-born, dragging behind him a piece of placenta torn from the primordial egg. It eventually settled in space and became the earth—flat, arid, barren and open to all the winds. Ogo set foot on this earth. He found a fonio seed and planted it. When the seed was touched by the blood of the placenta, it too became red and conceived impurity, the mark of Ogo's sin.

Ogo searched the earth high and low for his twin Yasigui, whom he thought he had taken with him. But he soon recognized the fact that his sister was still within the egg. He hastily returned to heaven to find her, but he arrived too late. Amma, hoping to repair the damage done by Ogo, had discarded the half of the egg in which he had been conceived, keeping only the other egg in which the second pair of twins remained. He entrusted them to Yasigui.

When Ogo appeared before him, Amma pointed his finger at him and uttered the fateful words: "You crave success, but you will never succeed. You wanted to be the first, but you will not. You wanted to be complete and pure, but you are incomplete and impure. Return to earth, where you will live in the form of a male fox. You were named Ogo. From now on you will be Yurugu."

Angry and resentful, Ogo returned to earth and became Yurugu, the pale fox. His impurity spread over the entire land, but he could not reconcile himself to disgrace. His distress upset the universe, and Amma took pity on him. He decided to give him a companion, a new creation. He seized the eggshell half still hanging in the void and transformed it into a rectangular ark. From it he withdrew the

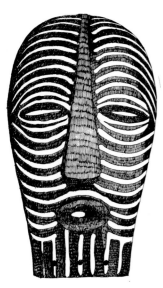

male twin and sacrificed it, resuscitating him as a man. He placed this new being in the center of the ark. He conferred on him the magic of water and speech and named him Nommo "he who offers drink." Next he created four new pairs of celestial twins and placed them in the four corners of the ark. Then he added all the animals and all the plants. When everything was done, he sent the magic ark to earth where Ogo was still wandering.

As the ark descended, the sun appeared, as did the moon and stars. When the ark took the form of the earth, the water—the source of life resulting from Nommo's sacrifice—transmitted its purity to the soil and fertilized it and four trees sprouted. Respecting the scheme devised by Amma, who wished humanity to multiply in a long succession of twins, the four couples of the ark united, each one giving his female to the male opposite him in the ark.

On the fourth day of creation, Yasigui, hoping to rejoin Ogo, descended to earth in the guise of a human being during an eclipse she had arranged. When she arrived, she found the red fonio seed her brother had sown, ate it and became impure. Enraged by the fate that had befallen her twin brother, she decided to avenge him by seducing Lébé-Sérou, one of the four males from the ark. She tricked him into eating the fonio seed, thus rendering him impure as well. He was unaware of this when he impregnated his own wife, thus transmitting his own impurity, which caused her death. From her corpse emerged a single child instead of the twins Lébé-Sérou expected. It was the effect of Ogo's curse, which next fell upon the three other sisters, then on all humanity, resulting in the loss of the twin births Amma had desired.

It is because of Ogo's sin and Yasigui's vengeance that women give birth to only one son or daughter. The Dogon deplore the fact that it is so seldom possible to respect Amma's primordial command: "Give double births in order to continue my work."

1. Scars around the navel and the blue color of their thick skirts are characteristic adornments of the women.

2. A council of the elders is about to take place in the village of Nini. The heads of families are gathering near the council house. The first man on the left is wearing the traditional Dogon bonnet.

3. When they leave their village to go to the town of Mopti or to the local market at Tireli (held every five days at the end of the Dogon week), the men sometimes wear cotton boubous and headgear purchased from other

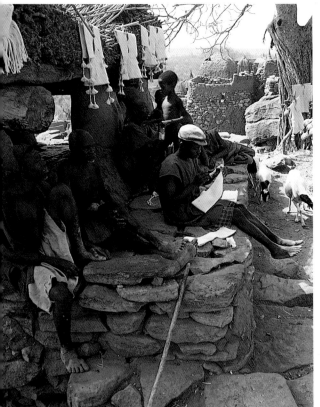

2

3

tribes—especially the Peul, whom the Dogons dislike but consider more "modern" than themselves.

4. While an old woman in the background separates cotton, others grind millet in front of a house made of banco (sun-dried clay mixed with straw). The upper story of this house is used for sleeping and storing valuables. Precious possessions are also often kept in granaries along with the grain. On the ground floor are stored various farming tools and cooking utensils.

1,2. To avoid encroaching on arable land, Dogon villages are built on rubble on the Bandiagara cliff above the caves formerly inhabited by the Tellem, "the red men" (2). Some of these caves still serve as cemeteries, but most are storehouses.

3. The houses are cubes of adobe, slightly trapezoid in shape, with flat roofs serving as terraces, a single door, and a few small apertures as windows. Most have only a one-room ground floor divided into three areas—for cooking, sleeping, and "living," with a corner

2

3

reserved for visiting friends. Next to their homes, the Dogon build their granaries, of the same materials. The floor is separated from the ground by a basement of stones and wood. The granaries are waterproofed with a clay coating. The only opening can be closed by a shutter, often decorated with mythical motifs. The conical roof is generally covered with thatch. While the roof must be replaced annually, the structure can last for ten or fifteen years.

1. *The baobab tree furnishes most of the wood for framework and floors. Its bark is used for insulation and also is an ingredient of medical ointments.*

2. *The council house,* toguna, *is forbidden to women. The branches piled on top protect the interior from the blazing sun. The very low ceiling obliges everyone to remain seated, on the theory that people generally rise when they are angry but remain calm when they are sitting down.*

1

2

3

4

3. When they can no longer be carried by their mothers, boys are given total freedom until adolescence. They spend their time at play in the communal care of the villagers, while girls help with the domestic tasks.

4. Upper and lower villages are connected by paths hollowed in the cliff. The long "staircase" in these rocks leads to the villages of Sanga on the high plateau.

1,2. Like the women, Dogon men prefer blue garments. The wide hats of plaited straw and boiled leather are theoretically reserved for heads of important families, for shamans or soothsayers.

3. The random placement of houses and granaries is deceptive. Actually, their location corresponds to both the heavenly domain and the human body. Each village, as a reflection of the body, is divided into quarters corresponding to a particular function: of farmers, carpenters, potters etc. . . . The smiths' quarter is at a distance, since these artisans, although respected for their healing talents, belong to an inferior caste.

1

Following pages: (1,2) Women of villages on top of the cliff (here, Ogol-the-high) have more contact with other peoples and tend to replace their traditional blue garments with printed cottons bought in Mopti.

While grinding millet, some women protect their chins from the repeated shocks of the heavy pestle as it pounds the mortar by tying a leather or fabric band under their lower lip.

1

WARANI

Ecuador

In the depths of the Ecuadorian forest live the few remaining survivors of an Indian tribe who call themselves Warani—"human beings" in their language. To their neighbors, they are *Auca*—"savages" in the Quechua idiom of the Incas, who gave them this name during their invasion of this territory many centuries ago.

Their reputation for ferocity and belligerence has persisted throughout the ages. But their existence was unknown to white men until 1956, when the world press reported the massacre of five American missionaries by "bloodthirsty Auca madmen." Any approaching stranger has always run the risk of a bloody incident. The latest one occurred in 1985 near the banks of the Cononaco, where oil-drill workers stole some turtle eggs, a delicacy highly prized by the Indians. In their defense, it must be said that most often such deplorable outcomes have been caused by the ignorance of white men who unwittingly violated some tribal taboo or disturbed the laws of nature so sacred to the Indians.

The origin of this tribe has never been determined. They may have moved down from the northern forests during the sixteenth century, driven by other tribes fleeing from the white man's invasion of the Amazon region. According to the most recent theories, they settled in the equatorial forests many centuries before the general withdrawal of the Indians before the Spanish invaders.

The Ecuadorian government has confined them to an Indian reservation in the northwest. Five hundred Warani, more or less half-breeds, live there today. Another 60 to 100 "true" pure-bred Warani survive in the deep jungle, where they are divided into four groups. Three of these groups are more or less sedentary. The fourth, composed of no more than twenty members, remains continually on the move, avoiding almost all contact with strangers of any kind.

The Warani ensure their survival and fill their days by gathering berries and fruit and hunting game. Only recently have they learned to construct canoes from tree trunks and to cultivate the soil.

The Warani believe in sorcerers who cast magic spells. They are convinced that the forest is inhabited by spirits. They believe that every misfortune is the result of some hostile wish and that it must be avenged. The slightest offense can lead to murderous reprisals. Their revenge may take years, but it is unavoidable.

Strangely, for a people so isolated and primitive, men and women are considered equals. They have the same rights of property, share in making decisions, and cultivate the crops on an equal footing. Only when a woman is pregnant or menstruating is she considered impure and dangerous, dominated by evil spirits.

The survival of the Warani, already so reduced in number, is constantly threatened, not only by outside factors, but by their own tribal custom of endogamy. Marriages are exclusively within the tribe; matings between sister and brother, even parent and child, are rapidly leading to their degeneration and their eventual extinction.

Beware of Women!

Waengongi created the earthly world. He fashioned a flat disk, surrounded by water and slightly raised on the side of the setting sun so that the rivers would flow eastward. He then covered it with a vast forest and placed animals and men inside it. This world was an exact replica of his own. Everything living in the earthly forest also lived in the celestial jungle. The only thing different was time, which was limited for the creatures below, eternal for those who lived on high.

One day Waengongi, after cutting trees, planting, fishing and hunting in his heavenly domain, hooked his hammock to the stars as usual. After drinking *tepae,* he fell asleep. Suddenly he was awakened by the "animal master," who was very angry. "The earthly tapir has come to me complaining, 'Man has struck me with his arrow but did not kill me; he only made me suffer!' Then it was the bird and the fish who complained to me. I have therefore decided to remove all game from the human hunting grounds."

Waengongi, who had listened attentively to the complaints of the animal master, succeeded in pacifying him with words. Then he said, "I will give men a subtle poison, *oonta,* to use for hunting. They will kill the animals they need for food rapidly and without making them suffer." The animal master was to verify that man respected Waengongi's wishes and, if necessary, punish those who disobeyed. For a while everything went according to his wishes. Men hunted only the game they needed for food, and thanks to the *oonta,* animals died without suffering. But soon everything went wrong. One hunter, returning home, set his blowpipe on the floor along with the quiver holding his poisoned arrows. While he slept, his wife, who was indisposed, therefore impure, approached and touched the weapons. The next day the hunter returned to the forest. He spied a monkey. He adjusted his blowpipe and let loose; the arrow struck the monkey but did not kill it. The monkey ran away and showed his wound to the animal master. Furious, the latter decided to give a warning to men: he sent them the *ononqui,* minor maladies. Suddenly afflicted with chills and fevers, the men could not understand what had befallen them.

Another hunter, tired from much tracking, returned home and stretched out on his hammock beside his wife. The next morning he returned to the hunt. He spotted a stag and struck it with his lance. Twice he wounded it, but was unable to kill it. The stag escaped and showed its wounds to the animal master. Enraged, the latter sent to earth the *wenae*, serious maladies, messengers of the evil spirits of the air. Men could not understand what was happening when they were struck down by sudden death.

A short while later, three young hunters whose mothers were indisposed or pregnant attacked the anaconda, Obe, who at that time was merely a tiny serpent. The first boy fired an arrow, which struck the serpent. Instead of dying, it began to swell. The second boy wounded it with his lance but did not kill it. The serpent swelled even bigger. When the third boy's arrow struck Obe, he became enormous and attacked the three hunters, who ran off screaming in terror.

Then the animal master appeared, beside himself with rage. "Men," he said, "in your ignorance and heedlessness you have permitted impure women to destroy the *oonta*'s magic power. You have disobeyed Waengongi's orders by causing animals to suffer. From now on, Obe will be your punishment. As long as you live on earth, the giant anaconda will pursue you relentlessly and try to devour you. And when you die and hope to swing in the hammocks among the stars beside Waengongi, a second Obe, a celestial one, will lie in wait for you. In order to escape into the celestial forest, you will have to leap over him and show yourselves to be light enough so that he cannot catch you. But the more suffering you cause to animals on earth, the heavier you will become . . . and Obe will be sure to catch you!"

That is why the Warani carefully avoid the swamps in which the anaconda lurks, and never permit an indisposed or pregnant woman to approach their weapons.

2,3. In this blue-green universe of the equatorial forest and the meandering Cononaco River one of the three semi-sedentary groups of Warani lives. This impenetrable jungle gets such frequent downpours that it has been given the name "rain forest."

1,5. A village on the Cononaco where a small clan of some thirty persons live. The seven adult men are able to provide sustenance for all.

4. A canoe carved from a tree trunk. The Warani learned to navigate the rivers only six years ago. Until then, they were afraid of disturbing the water spirits—a superstition in which some still believe.

2,3,5. The Warani exploit the resources of all three levels of jungle vegetation. On the ground, they use lances to hunt peccary and deer which seek the shade of trees. In the trees at forty or fifty feet above the ground, they gather fruit and catch small climbing animals. At 115 to 200 feet, they find vines and the largest branches of giant trees. This is also the haven of all kinds of birds and monkeys, who are practically invisible, invulnerable to all but the most sharp-eyed, expert hunter with his blowpipe. This weapon is usually made from chontawood or a thick, stiff palm branch split in half and hollowed. The two hollowed channels are continually compared to make sure they correspond exactly, before being tied together with vines and finally polished smooth. These nine-foot-long weapons are most precise at a target distance of over sixty meters vertically and one hundred meters horizontally.

1

2

3

1,4. In order to retrieve a wounded animal or sloth (1) hidden or stuck in the high branches, the hunter climbs the tree with the aid of a rope of plaited vines attached to his ankles. The bamboo quiver on his back holds poisoned arrows. The black-dyed gourd contains kapok which, wound around the base of the dart, has the same ballistic effect as feathers.

6,7. For fishing in the swamps infested with snakes and crocodiles, the Warani employ barbasco, a vegetable poison that kills the fish within a small area when it is poured into the water. Only recently they have begun to use nylon lines given to them by Ecuadorian soldiers patrolling the Cononaco. Their catch usually consists of enormous, bony piranhas.

1,2. *A family prepares to cross a swamp near Yasuni. They listen attentively to the sounds of the forest, particularly to the birds, whose cries—or the absence of cries—could signal dangers: among others prowling these places is the giant anaconda, which can be twenty-six feet long.*

1

2

3. At nightfall, the men return from hunting to reenact the day's events before the women and children who have been cultivating yuca (manioc) and sweet potatoes in small forest clearings. The perilous jungle environment creates a strong sense of solidarity in the group, where everything must be shared, known, and accepted by all.

1. *Strong fibers are obtained by shredding vines, drying and then soaking them in vegetable solutions. They are then used for weaving hammocks. The finished article is dyed with a brown fruit sap that repels insects and prevents rot, which attacks everything in this climate. Next to the young girl are metal pots and pans gleaned from camps abandoned by European oil prospectors.*

152

3. Arrows are coated with oonta, a mixture of curares, causing temporary or permanent paralysis of the respiratory muscles when it enters the bloodstream. Some curares are used to immobilize prey for capture; others, to kill game or enemies. Curare is prepared in the home—except where there is a pregnant or indisposed woman, whose presence would render the poison ineffective. Cuttings from a special vine are soaked in an upright palm-leaf cone filled with water. A brownish liquid flows through the point into a gourd below. As it dries, it blackens and forms a thick scum which is removed and slowly cooked. The resulting sticky paste is curare.

2. Kempede, chieftain of a clan living near the Cononaco.

4. Nyama, Kempede's son, is the best hunter in the village. He is feeding yuca to the pet parrot he keeps tied in front of his hut.

5. Nyawade is Kadowe's second wife and his widowed sister-in-law. It is customary for a widow and her children to be taken over by the man of the family best equipped to provide for them.

WASHKUK

Papua, New Guinea

Twenty-five hundred Washkuk form part of the Sepik River population. Descendants of the last wave of Negroid migrations which reached the coasts of New Guinea between 3000 and 1000 B.C., they were first discovered by German explorers in 1895.

The social structure of their community, like that of all the other tribes related to the Sepik, is based on a division into two separate but complementary parts. Not into good and evil, as in so many tribal cultures, but into masculine and feminine. Each has its own rites, taboos and ceremonies, from which the other is excluded. There is no implication of imposing male supremacy. On the contrary, each sex is considered equal, simply different—differences that the other cannot understand. For example, the men believe their women are endowed with magic powers which they themselves can acquire only after long and arduous rites. So the women practice magic, while the rites of ancestor worship are the prerogative of men. When the Washkuk wish to consult the spirits of their ancestors, only the men are permitted to assemble in the spirit house.

Ghosts and spirits are ever-present in their daily life. Should fire break out for no apparent reason, strange noises be heard during the night, malady strike, harvests yield less than expected . . . obviously some evil phantom is haunting the village. It can be ensnared, or at least driven away, by the performance of complex ceremonies, the use of magic signs and traps.

In spite of the respect their art of magic inspires, women are considered impure, and are therefore excluded from the sacred gardens in which yams are cultivated. The sweet root vegetable has a special social and even mystical significance for the Washkuk. Only the purest of men, those who have not indulged in sexual relations within the preceding six months (the gestation period of the yam plant), are permitted to enter the sacred garden and tend the crop. Once harvested, the yams are exchanged during a special ceremony. After a number of complex agreements and contracts have been concluded, the two parties engage in a virtual competition to see which one can offer the greatest number of yams, the most magnificent specimens, to his partner. The prestige attached to this ceremony is so great that the loser of the contest is dishonored, occasionally to the extent of having difficulty in finding a woman willing to be his wife.

All children are considered female until the age of puberty. At that time secret rites and an initiation ceremony confirm the sexual identity of the child. As it often does in tribal rites, blood plays a symbolic role. For a girl, it is a matter of the first sign of menstruation. In the case of a boy, a cut is made in his sexual organ with a sharpened stone: blood flows from it for the first time—and, what is important, for the last. Thereafter, he is a man.

Like many of the neighboring indigenous tribes along the Sepik River, the Washkuk have developed an original style of art, generally inspired by their initiation rites. The fame of their sculptures and masks has spread far beyond the boundaries of the territory of New Guinea.

The Law of the Strongest

Man and woman were the last creatures to appear on our earth. In the beginning there was only flat, dry, barren land. Then the great ancestors created rivers, mountains, forests, and animals. And finally human beings.

At that time, man was not intelligent because his soul was empty. Woman was wise in mystery and magic because she had made an alliance with the air spirits. But she bore the mark of her original impurity, for at each moon she lost her blood.

By the river, Iwayawa, the man, built a hut and lived alone in it. On the edge of the forest, No-Kae, the woman, built her own, near to the altar of the souls. Nearby grew a beautiful black tree which she tended carefully every day. When it came time for magic, she cut the largest branch and in the darkness of her home she hollowed it to make a *garamut,* a long, slotted drum. From the highest branch she fashioned a stick and with it struck the drum. Every evening she played the drum and her powers increased. She learned the secrets of what is auspicious and what is not.

In his hut, Iwayawa was intrigued and disturbed by the sounds that reached him. Every morning he asked No-Kae what it was that she had been doing the previous evening. She always replied that she had done nothing—he must have been dreaming. One day he could no longer contain his curiosity. Overcoming his fear, he approached the woman's house when she went to the river for water. He went inside, saw the drum and stick, and took them back to his own house.

When No-Kae returned, she noticed the theft at once and screamed. She questioned a bird of paradise who had witnessed everything and told her in detail of Iwayawa's intrusion and thievery. She then ran to his hut and found him sitting inside. "Man, you have taken the sacred drum and stick," she cried. "Give them back to me at once!" Iwayawa began by denying everything. When the woman persisted, he got angry: "Woman, stop screaming! The noise of your *garamut* was too much for my ears. I know how to draw melodious sounds from it. You do not. And because I am stronger than you are, I warn you: if you return to bother me I will kill you." Whereupon he picked up a stone and threw it at the woman, who left . . .

Much later, they must have become reconciled, because they gave birth to a son and a daughter. The children lived in their mother's hut, but the boy visited his father every evening. In the meantime, the man had mastered the magic of the drum and was able to converse with the air spirits who fertilized the earth and protected his property. The man had planted yams, which he tended carefully. But they were wasting away day by day. The woman had planted taro in her garden, and she reaped a fine harvest. Suspicious, Iwayawa questioned his son, who finally confessed that he had passed his father's secrets on to his mother and that she was casting a spell over his garden. The father flew into a rage and struck his son on the nose. A few drops of blood spattered the yams . . .

The next day Iwayawa noticed that his yams were doing better. He inferred that his son's blood had partly exorcised the mother's evil spell. He summoned the woman and boy and said: "Woman, you are impure and the blood you shed each moon is proof of it. Son, you are impure through the fault of your mother. You resemble her too much, although you do not shed blood each moon. You must do so one more time, then you will come and live with me."

He raised his hand to strike his son's nose again, but the boy fled screaming into the forest. In his rush he scratched his penis on a low branch. Blood flowed, and Iwayawa's son thus had his first and last menstruation. For the first and last time, he resembled his mother. When his father found him, the blood had ceased to flow. Iwayawa then decided to take him home with him, for he had become a man.

Since then, the bleeding ritual of the Washkuk, as in most of the middle Sepik region, has been a means of clearing the impure blood from a young boy's sexual organ, separating him forever from the world of women.

1. *The basin of the middle Sepik River is a vast complex of swamps drained by a myriad of canals and river branches, like the Asinna (1). The sole means of navigation is the pirogue, a hollowed tree trunk. The crocodile head carved in the prow is a magical means of scaring away those dreaded reptiles.*

2,3. *Women of a Kuoma clan adorned for a ritual festival in front of the* haus tambaran *(house of the spirits) during the yam harvest. Women are barred from the* haus tambaran *as well as from the yam fields, but they are allowed to participate in certain festivities with the men, to bear arms with ritual motifs, and to dance in front of the* haus tambaran.

2

3

1,2,3. The tribes along the Sepik are famous for the quality and originality of their art. In the lower Sepik their art is becoming influenced by tourism, but in the middle and upper Sepik one still finds authentic ritual works with magic properties. All images of spirits and bygone ancestors are believed imbued with mystical powers, especially objects depicting stylized faces and expressions.

Their art is not intended to represent reality, but to depict supernatural beings. Some of their works, especially statues, are placed under their homes in order to protect them (1). But the sacred objects, such as masks, hooks, flutes, and long slotted drums, that the men use when they consult the great ancestors (2,3) are found in the haus tambaran, concealed from women and the non-initiated.

1

2

combinations of small and large cowry shells. Although the price of cowries has diminished since the introduction of official coins, they retain a certain value and are still considered signs of wealth. The grasses tied around their arms symbolize the supernatural aid of the forest spirits.

2. A cassowary bone inserted through the nasal membrane, and two "horns" of cassowary bone piercing the tip of the nose, are ritual "jewels" seldom seen.

7

9

8

1,2,3,4,5. An exorcism rite of the Nukuma clan. Various events such as noises, fires, or sickness having convinced them that the village is invaded by demons, the inhabitants have decided to chase them away. After seeking counsel from the "great ancestors" and aid from benevolent spirits in the haus tambaran, *the men lead the softly chanting women down the central lane of the village, menacing and insulting their invisible en-* emy. *To the sound of drums* (kundu), *they drive the demons to the lake, where they embark in two pirogues (1,2) to pursue them into the deep waters where the demons will drown —water being fatal to them.*

The young girl (3) and boy (4) are participating in this rite for the first time. Like the men, the boy wears on his chest a mask of plaited fibers decorated with cowry shells, affording magical protection.

1

2

3

4

5

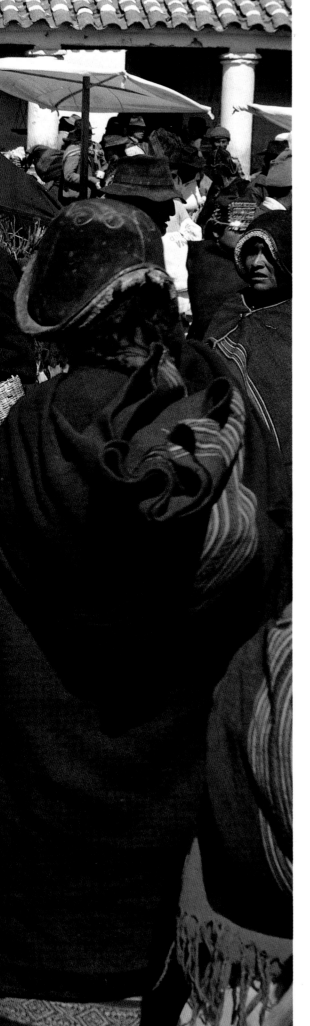

TARABUQUEÑOS

Bolivia

Periodically, the question of the origin of the sedentary populations of the Andes is reexamined and new theories are proposed. Did they come from Amazonia? from Asia? Polynesia? The most widely accepted theory to date is that Asian populations crossed the Bering Strait some twenty thousand years ago and then spread throughout the American continent. At the time their descendants reached the Peruvian coast, the region was covered by forests full of animals. By 10,000 B.C., the climate had radically changed. The forests had become a desert and its inhabitants were forced to move toward the Andes Mountains.

Several successive civilizations originated there, among them the Quechua tribes, one of which gave birth to the Incas. During the sixteenth century, the Spanish conquest crushed the formidable Inca empire which had dominated an area nearly 2,000 miles long, from the southern border of Colombia to the center of Chile and Argentina. A few groups survived outside of Peru, in Ecuador and Bolivia, among them the Tarabuqueños of southern Bolivia. They settled near a village called Tarabuco, from which they take their name.

Their pre-Incan origins are still evident in their daily life and particularly in their religious observations. Officially converted to Catholicism, they respect the Christian rites, but only superficially. For example, August 15, the date of the Assumption of the Virgin Mary in the Catholic calendar, is an occasion of great festivity. But in their hearts, the Tarabuqueños honor their own Mother Goddess, the source of life and protector of their crops. During many of their festivals they wear grotesque masks representing white men, mocking them with grimaces and ridiculous gesticulations. Proud of their descendance from the Incas and basically xenophobic, they await the day when their god, Viracocha, will return to deliver them as he has promised to do. In the meantime they celebrate with particular zealousness the *Carnaval* of March 12, the anniversary of the Indian revolt against the Spaniards in 1816.

Their distinctive costume is famous throughout South America. Their magnificent ponchos of wool are woven in many colors. The men braid their long hair in a pigtail, symbolic of their divine origin, and on their head, they wear a hat reminiscent of the helmet of the conquistadors.

Tradition, work, honor and observance of tribal customs are the virtues they respect and practice. Chores in the home and labor in the fields are fairly divided between men and women. The sexes enjoy equal rights and equal obligations—although the men alone decide, in council, the rules of the community. Their lands, used for agriculture as well as for raising cattle, are community-owned, periodically redistributed among the members of the tribe.

The Tarabuqueños are sober in their habits. They have never succumbed to alcoholism, which has ravaged so many other mountain peoples. They do, however, consume enormous quantities of coca leaves to combat the *soroche*, mountain disease, and the coca enables them to work longer and more efficiently on a minimum diet.

The Armadillo, the Cock, and the Man

The quarrel between Killa, the star of the night, and Inti, the star of the day, had just been settled. Jealous of his sister's beauty, the sun threw a handful of burning embers in her face, causing the scars that we can see today. A long battle ensued. Finally, after many efforts by the other gods, Pachacamac, "the first god who lives in the air," succeeded in reconciling brother and sister.

All the gods prepared to celebrate the new peace. In their joy, they invited earthly beings to join them. And so all living creatures here below, men and animals, set to work preparing their most beautiful attire.

In all the excitement, three creatures were in a quandary: the man from the high plateaus, the cock, and the armadillo. They didn't know how to dress for the occasion. Seated before his house, the man moaned, "Tay tay, tay tay! I have nothing to wear, no money, no cloth, not even an idea! I'll never be able to attend the festival. Everyone will mock me!"

K'anka, the cock, desperately paced around his courtyard, saying, "With what garment can I cover my bare body?" because at that time the cock did not yet have feathers. Nor did Kirkinchu, the armadillo, have a shell. Like his unhappy friends, he racked his brain, in vain. Then he suddenly had an idea. He asked the llama for a little wool and started to knit himself a coat. He started by knitting tight little rows. Time flew, and Kirkinchu began to panic. His garment would never be ready in time! So he decided to hasten the work by knitting more coarsely. Soon the coat was finished. What an astonishing coat it turned out to be! It was an uneven garment made of little scallops near the neckline and big ones in the back. But the color of the llama's wool was very drab.

In the meantime, K'anka the cock also found a solution to his problem. He noticed the mass of *ichhu* grass growing on the high plateau, cut some, placed the shortest on his back and sides and the longest on his wings and tail. He was dressed up! But the yellowed grass was rather faded and, like the armadillo, the cock deplored the drabness of his dress. At least both of them would be appropriately attired.

Such was not the case of the man, who was still prostrate before his house, filling the air with mournful cries, "Tay tay, tay tay."

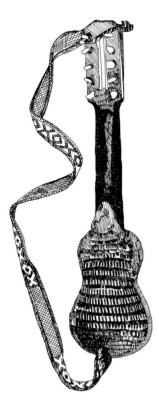

Pachacamac heard him and took pity on him. On that day of celebration everyone should be happy, he thought, so he asked the stars to help the man. Each of them gave him a ray of their light: Inti gave its golden yellow, Killa pure white, Qoyllurkuna (the luminous stars), red and orange. The other gods completed the harmony of these shades. Pachacamac assembled the sparkling rays in an immense arch which he sent to earth, after having washed it in a heavy rain.

The man, who had sought shelter in his house when the storm broke, went out as soon as the rain had stopped. To his amazement, he discovered a magnificent shimmering bridge connecting earth and heaven. Inspired by the will of the god, he rushed to the arch of light, seized an end and wound it around himself. Seeing this, K'anka and Kirkinchu also wished to benefit from the gift from heaven. The cock was quicker, shoving away the armadillo, he plunged into the rainbow as it began to disappear and emerged proudly, wearing a brilliant multicolored plumage. The armadillo stumbled in a mud puddle and only got to his feet in time to see the rainbow disappear. The man and the cock strutted around in their new clothes. Kirkinchu looked at his own coat: spattered with mud, it had hardened to become the grayish shell we know today. Disgusted, he threw it away. The man picked it up. Kirkinchu began to feel cold and asked for it back, but the man refused. Their dispute became so violent that it reached the ears of Pachacamac, who intervened again. It was decided that the shell would be returned to Kirkinchu, but that when the armadillo died, the man could use it as he pleased. The celestial festival could begin at last!

This is why the cock has such magnificent plumage, why the Tarabuqueño wears a "rainbow poncho" and plays music on a *charango* made from an armadillo shell.

1,2. East of Sucre, the ancient capital of Bolivia, at an altitude of almost 3,000 meters, is found "the cracked land," as the Indians call it. The cones and crevices of its surface are the result of intense underground volcanic activity.

3. While there are a few villages, most families live in small groups of scattered farms, surrounded by communal fields. The houses, cattle pens and grain stores are surrounded by low stone walls, painstakingly built in the traditional Andean manner. Another tradition is to bury a llama fetus in the foundation of the house to bring good luck to its inhabitants.

1

2

3

1,2. Household chores are women's work. On their looms, they weave material for ponchos and unku, *the latter made from two pieces of cloth stitched together and gathered at the waist. It is worn over a shirt (*kunka unku—"upper unku"*) or trousers (*siki unku—"lower unku"*). Under a poncho in the winter, the* unku *keeps the chest and back warm. The women's dress is the* almilla: *Several pieces of cloth are assembled to form a calf-length sleeved garment, often decorated with an embroidered band at the hemline. A short vest worn over the belt completes their outfit.*

1

3. The dry season lasts eight or nine months. The rest of the year rainfall is very sparse, so the water problem is of prime importance. The Tarabuqueños have forgotten the arts of their ancestors, who were past masters in terracing and irrigation. They cultivate as best they can cereal grains (wheat, barley, corn), vegetables (cabbage, onions), and above all potatoes, which are perfectly adapted to the climate. After fulfilling their immediate needs during the harvest season, they store a portion which they expose to the night frost, then to the sun's rays. Crushed in presses to extract the water, the result is a blackish substance, dehydrated and light, thus easily transported, which keeps well and constitutes a nourishing food all year round or in case of a lean harvest. Like everything concerning potato culture, this custom is inherited from the pre-Columbian populations of the Andes, who were the first to cultivate the potato plant.

1. *Men wear a traditional long pigtail, a sign of their noble origin—they claim to be direct descendants of the Incas, sons of the divine sun. Their headdress, the same as that of many of the women, is leather covered with black felt, the montera. Its shape resembles the helmet of the conquistadors. On feast days they wear a more ornate one, the ikachaska (flowered montera).*

5. *This young girl wears the "unmarried" hat, proclaiming her availability for marriage. Made of coarse wool and decorated with rows of beads, it is called a joq'ollo (tadpole).*

4. *Soft colors are traditionally reserved for children, bright ones for adults. This baby is dressed in pastel shades and wears a little lace bonnet which only rich families can afford.*

2,3,6. *Sunday is market day in Tarabuco. Its usually deserted narrow streets are crowded from the crack of dawn. Peasants wear their finest clothes and gather from fifty kilometers around. Whenever the men leave home, they carry a chuspa, a bright bag woven and sewn by their wives, who spend two or three weeks making one. Inside the*

1

2

3

4

6

chuspa *are coca leaves and a grayish substance produced from the ashes of a plant. As they chew the coca, they add a little of this paste to release its alkaloid. Coca chewing, prevalent throughout the Andes, is a means of alleviating fatigue, pain, hunger and, perhaps, of forgetting the sad plight of the Indians. The color of the poncho indicates social status and wealth and even the origin of the wearer. Warm shades (red, orange, yellow),* separated by black stripes, are the traditional ones; the colors' intensity varies according to the altitude in which the ponchos were woven. For example, those of Candelaria, famous for its weavers, are far deeper in color than those of Presto, a lower village. Some villages prefer a red poncho decorated with a brightly striped band. Predominantly black ponchos combined with various shades of blue, gray and violet are mourning attire.*

1,2. Market day in Tarabuco and numerous festivals (here at the village of Molle May) are occasions for the women to display their finest clothes. The crown of their pagoda-shaped festival headdress (montera) is covered with silver paper and decorated with metal disks, beads, bells. Men and women enjoy equal rights in Tarabuqueño society. The women's opinions are heeded, they have their say in decisions affecting the community and are fully in charge of educating the children.

1

2

IFUGAO
Philippines

In the light of today's knowledge and recent discoveries in paleontology, it is estimated that the first human populations to reach the Philippines 30,000 to 15,000 years ago were of the Australoid and then the proto-Malayan type. Several thousand representatives of these people remain in the archipelago. Subsequently, about 7,000 years ago, explorers arrived in continuing waves of migration. Initially they set up on the coasts, driving out the inhabitants, and finally ventured farther and farther inland before the arrival of new invaders. Most of these migrations were of Indo-Malayan origin. Toward the first or second century A.D., new Malayan peoples from Borneo appeared, introducing iron and the cultivation of irrigated land. The present population of the Philippines is thus a mixture of all these ethnic groups. The Ifugao are no exception to this rule and we may consider that their ancestors arrived and mixed with the populations who were living in the mountains of the north of Luzon Island in the third century A.D.

The term Ifugao means "inhabitant of the known world" and it is related to the Ifugaos' "pentamerous" (on five levels) concept of the world. At the top is Kabunyan, composed of four superimposed heavens. Just beneath is Pugao, "the known land"—i.e., the tribal territory. Lower still is Dalum, the lower world (also comprising several layers) which rests on the central pillar Kagah-na. Finally, there are Lagod, "the unknown world downstream" (a part of the lower world) and Daiya, "the unknown world upstream" (part of the upper world).

The Ifugao pantheon is one of the most vast known to man. There are more than thirteen hundred gods, genies and spirits, all specifically associated with a particular activity, whom believers invoke by means of complex rituals. Thus there is a god of war, another of truce, and others of omens, problems of inheritance or property, thunder, wind, rain, lightning, weaving, fishing, hunting, agriculture, various diseases . . . On the other hand, the Ifugao do not have a truly supreme god. Today these animist beliefs have more or less become a part of the ambient Christianity.

There is no real political or centralized system among these former headhunters. In their poverty-stricken society, there are three distinct categories of men. There are the Monbaga, whose prestige and material wealth make them natural arbiters in case of dispute. Of modest rank, the Natumok own a certain amount of land but not enough to be such important figures as the Kandangayan. The latter are rich landowners who are in a position to offer the community sacrifices of *carabao* (buffalo) or lend money.

Today, the official count of the Ifugao population is 70,000. In fact, few of them retain all their ancestral traditions nor are they of pure blood. Under the influence of missionaries, they go down into the cities where they mix with other populations and disappear into the vast melting pot of the Philippines.

A Curious Encumbrance

When men appeared on the earth, some time had passed since the gods who created the universe had returned to the four layers of heaven. Most of them had chosen to stay in the lower parts of the heavens called Kabunyan. All the gods felt that their task was finished. They were very tired, and educating men did not amuse them. They left this task to the most patient among them, Wigan-i-abunyan. Originally he was not a god, but he was immortal and his exceptional merits made it possible for him to live with his family among the gods. His wife Bugan-i-abunyan had given him two children, Kagibat and Bugan, who had contributed to the birth of the first human couple. In his great, compassionate heart, Wigan of Heaven wanted to help this odious human progeny, so ill suited were they to living. On his father's orders, the son, Kagibat, went off to join these human beings. He showed them how to make fire and construct huts, and then he taught them to fashion weapons to defend themselves and to hunt. Then he taught them agriculture and weaving. Finally he introduced them to the sacred ritual whereby they should venerate ancestors, gain divine favors, drive away evil forces and interpret omens. The men listened to him and followed his teachings. Soon, life on earth became easy and happy.

Kagibat stayed on with the men for a long time. He derived such pleasure from living among them that he even took one of their wives as his own. But it soon came time to return to the heavens. He took leave of his human friends, who attempted in vain to persuade him to stay, and despite their tears Kagibat left to rejoin his celestial family.

Once again among the gods, Kagibat related his terrestrial adventures. He did so with such enthusiasm that Bugan, his own sister, wanted to go down to earth. The daughter of Wigan of Heaven stayed with men for a long time. She taught them to use the forces of the air and water to their greatest advantage. Her work accomplished, she returned to the sky and in her turn gave the assembled gods an enthusiastic account of her stay on the earth. One of them, Gatui, a master in the art of mystification, listened to Bugan's words attentively. He had already heard Kagibat's story, but until then had paid no particular attention to the inhabitants of the earth, judging them unworthy of special interest. But when he saw all the gods become interested in men following the stories of the brother and his sister, he began to think that he had perhaps missed a good occasion to bring off a great farce. He turned toward his neighbor Kabunyan, the lower heaven. So loyal and trustworthy was Kabunyan that the gods had granted him the stars, the moon and the sun, which he bore in his breast. Despite these qualities, he was afflicted with a defect which all the gods ridiculed. Kabunyan was terribly curious! Each time there was an argument, an alliance or an affair in the world above, Kabunyan appeared out of nowhere, wide-eyed and breathless, invariably wanting to know all. Shrewd Gatui thus had no difficulty in convincing Kabunyan to go see the earth for himself. Already quite excited by the account of Wigan's children, Kabunyan the fourth heaven descended.

First he went to hide behind the clouds to spy on the men. But from that height they seemed so small! Then he went a little nearer the earth, then a little nearer still. Finally he was almost touching the ground. For the men, this was the beginning of their troubles. They could no longer stand up straight and had to walk bent over. The tallest had to walk on all fours. They obviously could no longer work and famine appeared in the land. Worse still, the sun that Kabunyan had brought with him in his descent dried up the rivers and scorched the crops. The men wept, cried out and implored the heaven to go away. Some cursed him, others threatened to fight. But Kabunyan did not understand the men's language and thought that they were thanking him and celebrating his presence. The more they despaired, the more Kabunyan the heaven was convinced that the men were honoring him. Swollen with pride, he weighed heavily on the poor earth. Finally Nabale, an old woman bent by the years and who, for that reason, could more or less stand up alone beneath the celestial vault, began pounding rice in a mortar. She addressed the task with all the vigor of her feeble force, when suddenly the pestle struck Kabunyan. He jumped up and cried, "Be careful, old lady! You've hurt me!" Nabale, worn out by the years, was deaf; she did not hear Kabunyan's cry and her pestle struck the heaven again. "Old woman, are you doing this on purpose? If you do that again, I'm leaving." By way of reply, the pestle hit the heaven a third time. Furious and humiliated, Kabunyan rose at once and swore that never again would he come near such ungrateful and impolite people. As he left, he took the sun with him, and the men were relieved at last.

That day, say the Ifugao, marks the final separation of the earth from heaven, who so far has never dared to return. No Ifugao would dream of harming old women; on the contrary, they are held in great respect.

1,2,3,4. The Ifugao say that their ancestors built the first terraces in the mountains of North Luzon more than two thousand years ago. They are, in fact, probably somewhat more than three hundred years old. It has been calculated that the walls around the rice paddies, placed end to end, would be 11,400 miles long! Today the Ifugao continue to build terraces, using techniques that vary with the nature of the terrain. If it is rocky, they begin by hollowing out the top of the mountain and filling it with often narrow platforms. With the stones thus removed, they construct small walls whose cracks are filled with a chalk-base plaster. All that re-

1

2

3

4

mains is to fill each platform with earth and then proceed to the terrace below it in the same fashion until they have reached the valley (4: the region of Pot Pot). But if the soil is crumbly, they begin at the bottom and work up the length of the incline. In this case, they try to dig out the earth to reach the underlying rock, which is used as a solid base and which, if necessary, can be supported with tree trunks. Some terraces are wider than others (3: Sedam region). All construction and upkeep of the terraces is done by men (1). The women are responsible for sowing, planting and harvesting the rice (3).

1,2,3,4. Houses are grouped in small hamlets up and down the mountain slopes (2). The Ifugao house is made up of a single room about nine feet wide. This wooden chest (3), totally covered by a pyramid-shaped thatched roof, rests on four stilts encased in a base of stones or thick planks. One enters on a ladder, which is taken up at night or when the owner is away. The wooden circular pieces on top of the stilts keep rodents away—particularly rats, which are very numerous in these mountains (1). Rich families, those who have

1

2

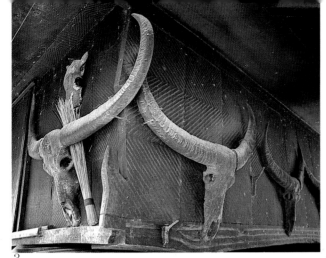

the means to give carabao *(buffalo) for sacrifice, hang the dead animals' skulls on the walls outside their houses as a symbol of social status. Also, paintings, sculptures and engravings (usually lines forming geometric patterns) decorate their walls (3). In the Ifugao society there is a class of aristocrats called* kandangayan. *In addition to their personal fortune, they exert moral influence among their people. A large hardwood bench placed against the stilts of one's house is the mark of his rank (1).*

3

4

1,2. *The Ifugao believe in anitos, spirits responsible for each individual's fate. During a special ritual for the anitos, the clan chiefs wear ceremonial headdresses displaying the tusks of wart hogs, symbol of strength and courage, and the beak of the calao, the bird considered to be the messenger of the gods (1). For coming-of-age ceremonies, monkeys' heads suffice, as the animals are held to be the privileged accomplices of the spirits, who are invoked with laughter and jokes. (2) An ex-*

3

ample of disappearing traditions: This old man is wearing a headdress made by his grandson. On top a monkey head is turned toward the sky, while according to magic custom, the skull must look in the same direction as the person wearing it.

3,4. During February and March the ulpi take place, during which one asks the gods for a good crop. People leave the rice paddies for several days while they stay at home, talk, smoke and drink palm alcohol (bayah). In July following the harvest, the apuy are celebrated. This is the occasion to thank the gods for having granted a bountiful harvest. The elders sacrifice chickens and study their blood (5). If the spirits are satisfied, the bulul (4), wooden idols with magic powers, are brought down from the granaries, which are connected with the house under the pyramidal roof above the living space. The idols are covered with the chickens' blood, thus making them responsible for the protection of the freshly cut rice which will be stacked in the granary.

4

1,3,4. The features of the Ifugao clearly show their Indo-Malayan origin. Small children, considered the principal earthly riches, are constantly in contact with their parents, who carry them until the age of two to three in scarves knotted around the body.

2. Various utensils are made by the Ifugao themselves, like these two women's wooden pestles and the stone mortar in which they are pounding rice. The shape is dictated by an ancient tradition.

4. The colors of fabrics are also determined according to ritual customs, each village having its own designs.

1

2

3

4

1,3. The men's favorite activity when they are not working in the rice paddies is hunting. Rodents, small mammals, and wart hogs are their main prey. They use three kinds of spears. One is used only for ritual dances and never leaves the confines of the village. The second, which they are never without when they leave home, serves as both a walking stick and defensive arm or, if necessary, a hunting spear (1). Its iron tip is small, unlike the very long spear with a "magic" shape designed to kill prey with ease. The latter is used

2

3

for big-game hunting (3). The hunter here is wearing a backpack of wart-hog skin, in which he keeps provisions.

2. On his expedition, the hunter eats mainly sweet potatoes, which are grown extensively in the mountainous areas. This crop is gradually disappearing and is being replaced by rice. The latter, however, did not arrive in the mountain areas until centuries after the introduction of the sweet potato in the Mountain Province.

JALE

Irian Jaya, New Guinea

Unlike the giant populations living in the mountains of New Guinea, the Jale, who inhabit the high valleys in the central chain of the Irian Jaya, in the Indonesian part of New Guinea, are only a little over four feet tall. But they are aggressive, combative, and involved in almost continual wars interrupted by rare truces. Ethnologists have observed the same phenomenon of permanent and extreme belligerence in other societies which, like the Jale, live in small, self-sufficient communities where young boys remain for an unusually long time close to their mothers in an exclusively feminine environment. Such conditions, they have found, produce particularly violent men.

In the case of the Jale, warfare is the usual means of settling all disputes. Revenge, for some offense such as the theft of a wife or even of a pig, is the principal cause of their conflicts.

They descend from the most ancient populations of New Guinea (40,000 to 10,000 B.C.), but they could not be more different from their neighbors. In addition to their tiny stature, the Jale are often pale-eyed, with reddish-blond hair.

The Jale live in villages of seventy or eighty family huts grouped around a central house, the residence of initiated men. This is a sacred place which even enemies respect. They may set fire to an entire village, but they never attack this final refuge of vanquished warriors. The family dwellings are inhabited by women, girls, and non-initiated boys. The boys leave this feminine environment around the age of twelve or thirteen, an event marked by a series of ceremonies signaling their detachment from the world of women and initiating them into the world of men.

Both men and women labor in the fields, but only men are entitled to hunt birds and game animals. The women trap insects, lizards and frogs. The domain of women is the earth, of men, the air. Any violation of the tribal code is punished by banishment from the community—tantamount to a death sentence in that part of the world.

Like many Papous, the Jale are very superstitious. They believe that the souls of the dead, be they friends or foes, return to haunt the living. Complex funeral rites, followed by cremation, are required in order to drive the ghosts away from the village. Moreover, superstition rather than savagery is responsible for much of the cannibalism still practiced by them in certain remote valleys. By eating an enemy, total vengeance is achieved; since his soul is swallowed they are thus annihilated. Cannibalism is also a means of absorbing the vital energy of an enemy and taking possession of his most formidable qualities. The Jale therefore eat the heart or liver of a warrior noted for his bravery, the legs of an indefatigable runner, the chest and biceps of an expert archer, the brains of a wise man . . .

Anthropologists propose a third explanation, almost a justification: In regions where game is scarce and available foodstuffs are limited to taro and sweet potatoes, human flesh may be a vital nutritional supplement to the meager diet of these primitive people.

The Ghost

Enemies had stolen four pigs and three women. During the punitive expedition that followed, the village lost two warriors, namely the fathers of Wariuk and of Borrongksini. The latter's father had fought valiantly and died combatting three enemy warriors. The glorious wounds on his chest gave evidence of his courage. Wariuk's father, on the other hand, had hidden in the bushes and, as he tried to run away, was shot in the back by two arrows. The shameful wounds were evidence of his cowardice. When the bodies were cremated, the soul-healer said, "The soul of Borrongksini's father grew greater in combat. It will be welcomed in the land of the ancestors. But the soul of Wariuk's father diminished in combat. It cannot be admitted to the land of the ancestors."

One night when Wariuk was sleeping in his hut with his two sons, he was aroused by smoke filtering through the log walls. He went outside, but saw no sign of fire. The next night he heard leaves rustling around the house, but there was nobody there. The third night, the hearth fire glowing in the center of the hut suddenly burst into flames so brilliant that it awakened Wariuk and his sons.

The next morning, Wariuk went to the house where his wife and daughters lived. He told them what had happened. Like all women, his wife was well versed in magic and prophecy. She understood at once what was going on, and she was very frightened. Trembling with fear, she told her husband that it was a manifestation of a discontented ghost.

Later, she fell ill; then her daughter, along with the other women of the village. Then the harvest was spoiled. The men failed to escape various plagues that fell upon the village. The soul-healer consulted the dead ancestors. The fire-father spirits revealed that the soul of Wariuk's father was prowling in the neighborhood. Unable to be accepted into the domain of the ancestors, he had become an evil ghost and was seeking revenge on his former friends. Moreover, he could also do everything he had been unable to do during his lifetime, like fly, breathe underwater, be in several places at the same time, walk through walls and speak to the souls of the living.

The soul-healer said that it was Wariuk who would have to find the solution. So Wariuk sacrificed animals and offered much of his harvest to his father's ghost. He even built a beautiful house, decorated with wood carving, beyond the village limits. But nothing worked. Misfortune continued to plague the community. Then Wariuk decided to try to frighten the ghost, scare him away once and for all. On the eve of the full moon, he hid at the edge of the forest and waited. Suddenly the ghost appeared. It was a barely visible shadow, with very long oily hair and a tongue hanging to the ground, covered with luminous spots. Wariuk stood up, screaming as loud as he could, and shot arrows in the direction of the evil spirit. The frightened ghost fled, skimming over the ground, flying noiselessly above the grass. Wariuk pursued it relentlessly. Seized with panic, the shadow in its headlong flight passed through a hut before disappearing forever into the forest.

Wariuk, in his desperate pursuit, followed the ghost into the hut, where he stumbled over the body of a sleeping man. It was Borrongksini. His soul, like those of all human beings during their sleep, had left his body. And it didn't have time to return to it before Borrongksini was so abruptly awakened. When he rose from his bed, the light had left his eyes. In scorching tones he cursed Wariuk. "Coward, son of a coward! You have made me lose my soul. I will take another from one of the members of your family." He disappeared into the night. Struck with panic, Wariuk moved with all his family and founded another village, a long way away.

Ever since then, all of the descendants of Wariuk's clan have known two things. It is dangerous to go outside the village at night because Borrongksini is still prowling there, and if one meets a warrior from Borrongksini's clan, one must slay him at once. Between the two clans, there is one soul too few.

1,3. The mountainside (its peaks soar to over 13,000 feet) is covered with incredibly dense jungle. Such rugged terrain is a protection for the Jale, but at the same time obliges them to walk for days on end in order to reach destinations merely a few dozen miles away.

2. The long móróal hut and its dependent buildings are nestled in the middle of the forest. Access is strictly forbidden to women and non-initiated men. The móróal is the most sacred, most secret ceremony of the Jale and takes place very rarely. The long hut, in which the "men of great knowledge" are isolated with the novices, must be built far away from the village in a secluded spot. On this

1

2

3

site are gathered together the konu, *a banana tree whose leaves are used in the ritual, and whose fruit is forbidden to women and non-initiated boys; the* pitmin, *a variety of wild sugarcane, whose extremely rapid growth is considered magical; and the* pōe *tree which, when burned, produces charcoal for blackening the novices' faces at the end of the initiation ceremony.*

4. Reaching dizzying heights above the torrents, covered bridges are built from thick tree trunks loosely tied together with vines, enabling them to withstand the frequent earthquakes and landslides. They are a favorite playground for the children.

4

1. *This woman is filling her gourds at a spring near Borrongkoli. The proximity of this region to the Baliem River Valley facilitates intertribal contacts, which sometimes influence the manner of dress. This Jale woman is wearing a skirt of long fibers, more typical of the valley women, instead of the traditional Jale garb of a short skirt of evenly chopped off fibers (like the women in photo 6, page 201).*

2,3,4. *The bag made of plaited fibers that men and women wear over their head is used to carry provisions of taros and sweet potatoes when they travel. After the boys' initiation (during the ceremony called wêt that takes place just before puberty), wild boar tusks, symbolic of courage, are inserted in a hole pierced through the nostrils—like this chieftain of the Kono clan. Or a bamboo stick is inserted through the nostrils; another thicker, hollowed piece of bamboo, decorated with ritual motifs designed to protect the warrior, is passed through the earlobe.*

2

4

3

1,4. Most of the men wear a long skirt of split rattan wound around their body. It is very tight over the stomach and around the waist and flares lower in the back, resting in front on a long penis sheath. When they move about, they lift the edge of their skirt (4). The warriors' preferred weapons are stone hatchets and bows. The former, crudely cut from flint, are formidably effective in combat, and are also used as a tilling instrument.

2,3. The distinguishing traits of the Jale are their small stature (4 feet, 9 inches on average), pronounced Negroid features, and the

1

2

3

surprising, inexplicable color of their hair and eyes. Like these two boys being carried by their mothers, most of the children have reddish blond hair, and many Jale have light green eyes (3).

5. This man is preparing a meal with the aid of a woman from the neighboring Dani tribe (recognizable from her braided hair), which is often at war with the Jale. Using a split stick as tongs, the man places heated stones on a bed of dampened reeds. The woman is covering the stones with a layer of leaves, on which sweet potatoes will be placed. The reeds are then folded over them to form a cooking pot in which the potatoes will be steamed. Despite their conflicts, a certain amount of commerce based on barter is carried on among the women of different tribes.

6. A group of women and little girls, visibly upset by the presence of a stranger, are standing before the large circular house of the men, to which entrance is forbidden them. One can see the edge of the roof, covered with casuarina bark.

7. A Jale dagger. Cut from a large pig bone, it has two lateral "teeth" that tear the victim's flesh when it is withdrawn with a circular movement of the wrist.

4

5

6

7

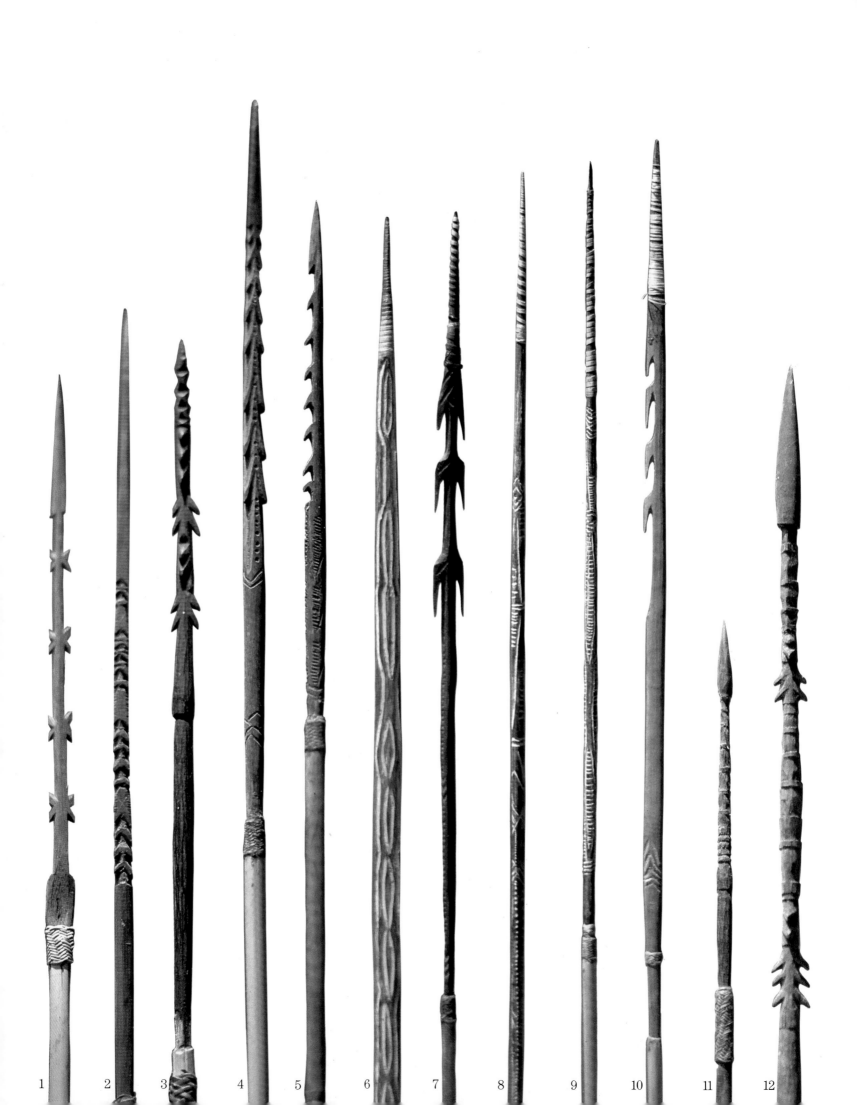

1 2 3 4 5 6 7 8 9 10 11 12

The Jales' arsenal of arrows is extremely varied. These (1 to 5) are used during combat between acquainted clans; their primary function is not so much to kill—although this may occur—as to wound.

Arrows are also used during tribal warfare (6 to 10). The barbs are longer and keenly sharpened; the tip is wound with rattan. When the arrow is withdrawn, the fibers remain inside the body, infecting the wound and causing certain and painful death. Some arrows are of ritual and magical value (11 to 15). These are used when avenging an ances-tor who has been humiliated by his enemies. The tip is made from a bird's beak and is designed to break off or literally screw itself (13) into the enemy's body.

Finally, arrows are used for hunting game (16 to 18). The blade is carved from a sliver of bamboo, sharpened on both sides.

19. Closeup of an arrow with a very long, thick bamboo blade, used for killing big game (boar and deer).

20. Closeup of a five-pointed sharpened arrow, designed for hunting birds.

13   14   15   16   17   18   19   20

LADAKH-PA

Indian Tibet

The Ladakh-Pa who live on the high plateaus of the Kashmir in northern India are related to the Tibetans, who are themselves related to the K'iang who inhabited southwest China long before the Christian era. Chinese expansion gradually drove the Tibetans toward the west and from the plains into the mountains.

During the eleventh century a group of these Tibetan emigrants, perhaps as a result of internecine wars or perhaps attracted by the "land where the sun sets," broke off from the others and headed west to settle in Ladakh. They found Indo-European peoples (Môns and Dards) already established there, most of whom practiced Buddhism in the form of Hinayana—"the small way"—which had been introduced by missionaries of King Asoka in the third century B.C. The new arrivals drove away much of the primitive population, and with the remainder created the ethnic strain from which the Ladakh-Pa descend. The Hinayana was supplanted by the beliefs they brought with them: Mahayana—"the great way." Devotees of Tibetan Lamaism, they are divided into the same two major sects that are found in Tibet: the Red Hats (faithful adherents of the teachings of Padmasambhava, who introduced Buddhism into Tibet); and the Yellow Hats (scrupulous observers of the laws of the Dalai Lama).

In this poor region survival was ensured by controlling the birth rate through a system of polyandry. Each woman was also the mate of her husband's younger brothers. The oldest son alone was permitted to marry; the children fathered by his brothers and his wife became his own. The second-oldest brother might aspire to one day marry his elder brother's widow, but for the younger brothers there was little hope. They became Buddhist monks, sangha. The entire system was, in fact, devised and supervised by the lamas and it functioned effectively for many years.

The equilibrium was finally upset by the population explosion of the Kashmiri, whose Muslim faith inevitably leads to a high birth rate. In quest of greater living space and attracted by the rich mineral deposits of Ladakh, these new immigrants have profoundly perturbed the previous demographic balance. At the same time, the Indian government appropriated the functions and authority of the lamas. The prolific polygamy practiced by the Kashmiri Muslims is leading to the disappearance of polyandry and a decrease in the number of sangha. Why should a younger brother become a monk when he is certain to find a wife? If not in Ladakh, at least in the valleys below?

The fairly recent demographic metamorphosis of their region is changing the life and traditional customs of the Ladakh-Pa. On these barren mountain plateaus with only two inhabitants per square kilometer, they are dying out. Their agricultural methods have remained extremely rudimentary; their few dzo (a cross between cow and yak) furnish insufficient milk; the Ladakh-Pa have no idea how to exploit the mineral resources of the subsoil.

The Indian army has built a civil and military airport at the foot of the monastery of Spituk, where monks retire for meditation. Organized groups of foreign tourists arrive by busloads . . . the Ladakh-Pa are rapidly approaching the setting sun.

Glory to Ge-sar!

Sickness, war and famine ravaged the earth. The kingdom of Glin was particularly plagued. The king had died and his ambitious heirs were killing each other in fratricidal combat. The wisest, oldest of the lamas, who had devoted his long life to meditation and prayer, succeeded in touching the heart of Buddha. Buddha promised him that a liberating hero would soon descend to earth to save the unhappy kingdom.

Shortly thereafter, Princess 'Cog-mo gave birth to a son she had conceived without ever having been touched by a man. A dream had announced to her that her son would have an exceptional destiny. She expected him to be tall and handsome, but he was an ugly infant. In spite of her disappointment she loved him, and she called him Jo-ru. When Khro-thun, the boy's maternal uncle, saw him for the first time, he burst into malevolent laughter and decided to do away with him. But the child was endowed with supernatural powers and he managed to elude all the traps his uncle set for him each day. In fact, every day Jo-ru turned the situation to his advantage, irritating Khro-thun. Realizing the hopelessness of his evil efforts, Khro-thun banished 'Cog-mo and her ugly son from the kingdom. They could return to Glin only when the boy had become of age.

So they left. After long and arduous travels, they finally found refuge in the land of Rma. Jo-ru grew up there and during his exile he accomplished a thousand heroic exploits, fighting off demons and saving kingdoms. But he remained as ugly as ever. During one of his expeditions he met a beautiful young woman, 'Brug-mo, who had since eternity been destined to marry the heir to the kingdom of Glin. Later, Jo-ru became the ruler of Rma. He grew stronger and wiser. He was beloved by his subjects, who reverently called him Jo-ru the Just. All the peoples of the region were under his rule.

He finally came of age and returned to Glin, where his uncle had installed a reign of terror. Through his spies, Khro-thun had learned of Jo-ru's coming. He made a pact with the devils of heaven and earth. If they would help him dispose of his nephew,

he would help them gain control of the earth. Khro-thun then proclaimed far and wide that the kingdom of Glin, its ancestral treasures, and the hand of beautiful 'Brug-mo would be accorded to the winner of a horse race between himself and Jo-ru. He prepared a treacherous course. It stretched out over the crests of the snowy mountains and the depths of the dark valleys, where ambushes could easily be set. All along the way, he posted his devil accomplices to waylay his rival.

Buddha came to Jo-ru in a dream and told him to send his mother and the beautiful 'Brug-mo up into the white mountain to seek a magic horse the gods would send him. The women found it and brought it back. It was called Rkyan-rgod. Thereupon, Jo-ru accepted his uncle's challenge.

At the beginning of the race, Khro-thun outdistanced his nephew because the devils at every mountain pass, at every summit and in every valley attacked Jo-ru, trying to unseat him and delay him. But the gods had given the hero the gift of ubiquity. He could fight and conquer in several places at the same time. His horse ran faster than the wind. And when Jo-ru began to weaken, there was always a monk, a man or a child to offer him water and urge him on. Finally Jo-ru caught up with his uncle, passed him, threw him to the ground and won the victory at the Pass of the Prayer. Immediately he was surrounded by the fire of heaven and began to blaze with light. His ugliness disappeared. He became a magnificent and handsome warrior.

All the people of Glin, rich and poor, who had helped him during the race knew that he was the liberator they had been waiting for. They admired his new appearance, and as 'Brug-mo ran forward to greet him, they changed his name to Ge-sar the Glorious. The entire world echoed with their joyful cries: "To the east, China is a mirror; to the south, India is a zodiac; to the west, Iran is a book; to the north, Ge-sar is an offering."

Since that time, the happiest and proudest of all the Ladakh-Pa are those who can boast of ancestors who were supporters of Ge-sar of Glin.

1. Situated at altitudes between 9,000 and 18,000 feet, Ladakh is a vast desert, arid and poor, with high mountains unsuitable for any cultivation. The extreme dryness presents inhabitants with water problems, not only in summer, when temperatures rise above 86° F., but also in winter, when the thermometer can drop to −40° F. Less than one seventh of the land is cultivated.

2

2. *Bundles of branches are attached to the roof and cloths printed with mantra, Tibetan religious incantations, are hung on them. It is thought that when the wind blows them, it constantly repeats the prayers of the faithful.*

3. *Houses are made of bricks of adobe—a mixture of clay and straw cooked in the sun. The façade is covered with a chalk-base filler. The roof is made of poplar branches and straw, covered with clay. It serves as a terrace for drying fruit and, in summer, for sleeping in the cool air. The kitchen and bedrooms are upstairs. The ground floor is used for storing hay and grain, and for stables.*

3

1,3. The prayer mill is the daily companion of the Ladakhi. It is made of copper and decorated with religious symbols in silver. Sacred texts are inscribed on fine bands which are rolled around a central axis. The mill is turned from left to right (to follow the cosmic movement) and says one's prayers as long as it is rotated. This has the double advantage of honoring the gods while leaving a certain liberty to the faithful.

2,4. Inside the houses of the poor (2) as well as those of the rich (4) stands the earthenware stove decorated with cast-iron plates, while on the shelves are displayed the carefully pol-

1

2

3

4

ished copper utensils decorated with silver—a source of particular pride among Ladakhi housewives.

5. In the isolated valleys like that of Zaskar, where the standard of living is lower, the house is often no more than a single large room. One part is used for cooking and the other for sleeping. The wife of the eldest son prepares the meals for all her in-laws. Here, barley seeds are being grilled and then will be pounded. The flour thus obtained is mixed with gurgur chaï *(salt tea with rancid butter)* to make tsampe *(called* kolak *in Ladakhi),* which constitutes the usual Tibetan meal.

1

2

3

1. *This monumental statue of the Buddha stands in the new temple built inside the monastery of Thiksey.*

2,3. Buddhism is widely practiced among the Ladakhi, whose community is divided between the Red Hats and the Yellow Hats, the two rival schools of belief. The numerous celebrations provide the occasion for the community to meet, particularly when it is celebrating the anniversary of a gompa, a monas- tery. *The peasants journey from the farthest valleys and dress in their most beautiful attire (2) to join in the celebration of the various religious services. The lamas and novitiates gather in the main courtyard. During the celebration of Angook in the monastery of Tak Tak (3) they communicate with the manas of former monks who have acceded to the divine sojourn.*

1. In a street in Leh, the capital of the Ladakh, this girl is selling cabbages and turnips. These vegetables, along with potatoes, were introduced to the Ladakh only twenty years ago. Today they are found only in the vicinity of Leh. Throughout the rest of the region, wheat and barley are cultivated, providing the daily food staple.

3,5. The tibi is the traditional headdress, worn by men as well as women. Its shape is inspired by ancient Chinese customs.

1

2

3

4

5

2,4. The perak *is the elegant headdress for women. Two panels of thick felt frame a strip of felt falling to the neck. A red cloth with polished turquoise stones covers the strip. Other stones, pearls, chains and silver medallions complement the headdress, and their profusion indicates the social rank of the woman's family.*

6. In the valley of the Zaskar, this old man is wearing the tibi *and the* kos, *a thick wool coat for winter. He is leading a* dzo, *a cross between a cow and a yak that is well adapted to the climate and altitude.*

7. Mani stones, covered with esoteric symbols and inscriptions in old Tibetan, are placed by the faithful on long, low walls near the monasteries or along paths. The faithful often cannot read the stones and rely on the lama's explanations of them. It is said that moving the stones brings bad luck.

6

7

BONDA

India

Adivasi is a composite word meaning "former inhabitants." It is the name given by the Indians to the oldest groups of aborigines still living on the subcontinent. Among them are the Bonda, of whom only eight hundred remain today.

More than three thousand years ago, the Bonda's ancestors retreated from the invading Aryans to seek refuge in the arid mountains of Orissâ, in India. The insignificant number of Bonda surviving today are of no interest to the government, preoccupied as it is with the problems of a tribal population of 45 million people. Scorned and ignored by the Indian government, they are despised by the other *adivasi* peoples who consider them to be dangerous savages. They are in part responsible for their inevitable extinction, given the combined effects of alcoholism, inbreeding, and violent behavior.

In an effort to protect their tribal populations, the Indian authorities have classified the Bonda as one of the "indexed tribes," a category of citizens that is part of the "indexed castes" and is composed of untouchables as well as persons without caste. This gesture of official good will has had dramatic consequences. The Bonda territory is administered by untouchables—people rejected by the upper castes and who at last find people who are "lower" than they are and on whom they can inflict the suffering and humiliation which they themselves must endure.

Could this be one of the causes of the Bonda's immoderate taste for *salap*, palm alcohol, and more recently for the denatured alcohols sold them by unscrupulous suppliers? The Bonda claim that *salap* helps them enter into contact with magic forces which enable them to accomplish extraordinary feats. They say they can hypnotize a tiger so as to strike him before he reacts, and force a snake which has bitten someone to return and suck his own venom out of the wound!

Bonda men and women are equals—in marriage as well as in participation in ceremonies. However, each individual has a precise place in the clan, and each clan its place in the village. Each person assumes the functions inherent to his place, in which he remains after death—in the "land of the great dead" where he will live eternally with his dead ancestors.

The Bonda see spirits everywhere—in the earth, the water and the air. They particularly worship those who live in the trees and plants. According to Bonda belief, most of these spirits are unfortunately not there to protect them but to tempt and abuse them, either out of pure spite or because a witch from an enemy village has prompted them. Even the beautiful goddesses of Bonda legends are irascible and vindictive. Sickness, death, and meager harvests are never due to bad luck but to evil brought about by a hostile spirit. The only remedy is a punitive action designed to break the evil charm and take revenge on the enemy. Despite the efforts (however discreet!) of the Indian authorities, such beliefs lead to a regrettable number of ritual murders in these remote regions of the mountains.

An Unwise Joke

It was so hot that day that the village of Mudlipada was slowly baking. The twelve Bonda brothers, seated beneath the great ceremonial tree, were drinking *salap.*

Of all the men, they were the favorites of Maha Prabhu, the Fire God. The god had begun by fashioning the stars that shone in the heavens. Then water had bathed the earth, which became covered with plants and trees. Then came the gods, the genies and finally the animals. The cosmic order was in place; all that was left was for Maha Prabhu to finish his work. He did so by creating men, weak and faithless though they were. But the god loved them— especially the twelve Bonda brothers. The men returned his love by worshiping the god and offering him sacrifices.

That day the heat had become unbearable. The twelve founding brothers asked the wife of the eldest to go to the sacred spring and bring back the water which flowed for the gods' good health. During this time, the brothers would be hunting. The eldest brother's wife combed her long hair with care, put on her most beautiful clothes and set out on the path to the fountain carrying a jug on her head.

When she arrived, she saw a goddess and her servants bathing in the cool water. The goddess was sitting in the spring, unclothed, with her back turned to the newcomer, whom no one had heard arrive. A stone rolled under her feet and the women turned to face the stranger. "Who are you?" asked a servant. "I am the wife of the eldest of the twelve brothers of Mudlipada." "What do you want?" inquired another servant. "I have come to fetch water to refresh the mouth of thirsty men." Then, looking at the goddess, the Bonda wife continued, "And you, who are you? Why are you bathing in the sacred spring?"

"I am the goddess of this fountain," replied the bather, who stood up and turned toward the newcomer. The Bonda woman saw a body which was perfect but completely nude, and which shone strangely. First she snickered, then burst out laughing. "Why are you laughing?" demanded the goddess. "Because you are naked and it is impolite to show oneself like this to strangers. You say you are a goddess and you exhibit yourself without clothes to a stranger. I am only a simple mortal, but I would never behave in such fashion."

The goddess flushed with rage. "Stupid fool! Proud idiot! You should have looked more carefully before you spoke! The silk veil surrounding my body is as fine as a spider's web and it shines like the sun itself because it was the sun, the master of fire and the creator, who gave it to me. You see?!"

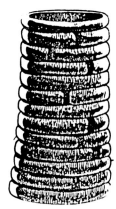

The goddess began to move and thousands of luminous streaks appeared on the light veil like so many blinding flashes of lightning.

The Bonda woman suddenly was very afraid. She fell on her knees and begged the goddess to pardon her. But the wrath of the goddess was unleashed. "Since you made fun of the sun himself, you will walk nude in the forest. May the top of you fly away, and your bottom disappear!" At once, the woman's hair parted from her head and her clothes from her body. Filled with shame and grief, she rushed to hide among the rocks.

Meanwhile the twelve brothers, who had been hunting, had returned to the village and found their wives—all except the eldest brother's, who had disappeared. A search party was organized and the wife was found, crouching in a dark cave and trembling. She recounted what had happened to her, and wept so copiously that the brothers understood the grievousness of her error.

The twelve brothers went to find Maha Prabhu. As he began to recount his misfortune, the eldest began to weep so uncontrollably that the god understood his difficulty. When Maha Prabhu's wife saw the man's tears, she took a strip of cloth 20 inches wide out of her own dress and gave it to the eldest brother: "Your wife and all the women of your people should wear this forever. They should always weave the same garment in the same size. The day one of them lets her hair grow or puts on another garment, your entire race will be destroyed."

Since then, Bonda women shave their heads and always wear the *ringa,* the narrow cloth skirt given them by the wife of the god.

1,4. In the forest-covered hills of the Orissâ, land ownership has always been a source of long and serious conflicts. Almost everywhere, warriors use tree houses to keep watch over the tribal territory while remaining sheltered from wild beasts. (Don't forget that there are still tigers here!)

2. The village of Mundlipada, considered the principal one of the Bonda country, consists of some thirty houses with bamboo walls and skillfully interwoven branches, standing on a foundation of stones and earth.

1

2

3

4

3. A woman returning from the fields walks by a small abandoned sindibor *overrun with weeds. The* sindibor *is a stone platform on which most religious ceremonies are celebrated.*

5,6. Rubbing a hardwood stick (male) against another of soft, split wood (female) heats and ignites the small chips in the split. Finally, one blows on the sparks using a small cone of leaves to start the fire.

5

6

1. The trees in certain places are reputed to be the haven of gods and genies. They are therefore not cut down. Other places are likewise preserved so as not to displease phantoms, furies or demons who would otherwise take revenge on the harvests. This is why the Bonda deforest only areas carefully delimited by their priests.

2. This man quenches his daughter's thirst with a refreshing drink made of salap mixed with water. Salap is a very strong palm alcohol which the men themselves drink straight. The young boy is introduced to salap when he is still at his mother's breast!

1

2

3

3. *Gathering edible plants and hunting were the only activities of the Bonda for a long time. Agriculture, linked to innumerable rituals and the cult of the gods, began to develop in the middle of the twentieth century. Rice, cereals and some cotton are the main crops. (Here, the region of Dumiripada.)*

1,2. On Sundays, Bonda women go down to the market at Mundaguda, a small Indian village built in the plain near the only road. They come to exchange their crops for manufactured products. During this time, the men who have accompanied them to the market begin getting drunk on salap. The number of metal rings around the women's neck and wrists indicates her social standing. The rings, regularly rubbed with oil, are of various diameters, with the widest covering thinner ones near the neck. The head, always shaved following an ancient evil curse, is capped with fine cords connected by strings of beads. The large circles of raffia pinned to the back of the head serve to cushion the heavy burdens carried by the women over long distances.

3. The Bonda have not mastered the art of pottery making. For them, the market is the occasion to purchase jars and pots. This woman is choosing a pot for honda, a kind of very sweet cake of which the Bonda are fond.

1,2,3. *Women's attire is prescribed by a whole set of taboos established by mythology. Apart from the shaved head, the body must be nude except for the hips, around which one winds a narrow cotton panel, the* ringa. *(This "primitive" dress scandalizes the puritanical Indians.) The thick strings of multicolored beads covering the chest indicate the husband's wealth. He takes pride in periodically adding a new string to his wife's jewels. The woman who, under the influence of*

1

2

the plains people, defies this set of customs is immediately classed among the dom, *the most impure people of all in the eyes of the Bonda, and she is of course rejected by her tribe. When the women go into the "civilized" zone, they cover their shoulders with a coat whose color and patterns are representative of their clan. The dyes used are often artificial, with the exception of indigo, which is considered a magic color.*

KARA-HAMAR

Ethiopia

The valley of the Omo in Ethiopia was discovered by several European explorers in 1885 and then forgotten. Apart from the Italian invasion in 1937–38, no white man had set foot in this isolated and arid land for almost a century. In the 1960s, anthropologists became interested in the region and made a sensational discovery there—not oil, not gold, but human bones dating from the Paleolithic period. They were contemporaneous with "Lucy," the famous fossil, almost three million years old, also discovered in Ethiopia.

Not far from the dig is Duss, the only village of the Kara. There are about 800 of these people, who differ from all the other nomadic ethnic groups of the Omo in that they have adopted a sedentary life of farmers and shepherds. They are directly related to the Hamar, who roam the swamplands bordering on Lake Turkana to their south. The two tribes are descendants of a very ancient indigenous population whose origin has never been determined.

The Hamar are exceptionally tall, with the men reaching an average height of 6 feet, 6 inches. But the Kara are even taller, standing 7 feet on the average. Their wives are of equally imposing height and are famous in all East Africa for their beauty, which is the pride of the entire tribe. The Kara are also proud of their skill in war, which for the most part consists of raids or skirmishes for the possession of water sources.

The social structure of the Kara and Hamar villages is that of the clans, with each one respecting its own taboos concerning food, sexuality and religion. The tasks of daily life are also assigned according to the clan. One is responsible for general administration, another for magic, a third for festivities and ceremonies, another still for the settlement of disputes. There is not a single chief, but a council of clan chiefs which makes all decisions. The shamans or witch doctors all have equal authority. They know how to make it rain on certain dates, how to cure diseases caused by evil forces and how to heal wounds and appease hostile genies.

Conscious and proud of their bodies, these beautiful giants pay particular attention to their coiffure. The Kara wear their hair pulled back in a long chignon which is held with clay and either decorated with ostrich feathers or painted in red, white and black—three colors of mystical and legendary significance. The Hamar prefer to bring their hair forward in a multitude of small braids. Both groups protect these works of art by sleeping on wooden neck rests, which serve as stools during the day.

The Kara men cover their body and face with cinders—a symbol of virility—for important festivities and the ritual combats between the clans which take place after the harvest. These ceremonial combats are of great importance because they enable the men to exhibit their beauty and courage and thus, perhaps, to attract a woman. The scars and lacerations, particularly those on the chest, are highly esteemed marks of valor.

The Magic of Colors

A very long time ago, when men and beasts spoke the same language, there were three great warriors in the kraal. They surpassed all the other men in height, strength and courage.

Kopirkulye, the first warrior, returned home happy. He had killed an enemy in battle and his song of glory could be heard afar. When he came to the kraal, he put his trophies down in front of his four brothers, told of his victory and went to sleep. But the next day one of his brothers had disappeared. He returned several days later, after having killed an enemy. He explained that a mysterious and uncontrollable force had pushed him to act thus. The same adventure befell the other three brothers, and then it was the villagers' turn. Kopirkulye did not understand the meaning of all this.

Nweite, the second warrior, returned home happy. He had stolen several cows in a neighboring village. He gave them to his wife and went to sleep. But the next day the cows had disappeared. Nweite went out to look for them and found them in the field where he had stolen them the previous day. He brought the cows again to his kraal. The following day, they had left again and he went out to look for them. The same turn of events repeated itself often. And Nweite did not understand the meaning of all this.

Karomeinda, the third warrior, returned home happy. He had gone into the enemy's country and had placed all kinds of terrible magic curses on them, wishing that their sorghum would rot on the stem and that their kraal should burn. He related his exploits to his family and went to bed. But the next day, the sorghum in his own field began to yellow and shortly the young shoots died. The next day, his house burned. These strange things happened almost all over the village, causing despair among the inhabitants. And Karomeinda did not understand the meaning of all this.

Day in and day out, misfortune continued to weigh on the village. The three warriors resolved to seek the advice of Nu-imba, the founder of the kraal and master of the fields. *He* would know what to do! He lived far from the village in a hut of branches which he had built on the flank of a mountain. Informed of the situation,

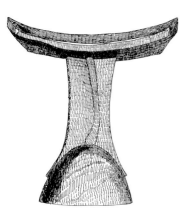

Nu-imba went behind a large rock, where he performed a number of magic rituals and, through the sacrifice of goats, he invoked the spirit of the "great fire father," the primordial *nu-imba.* He saw and he understood. When he returned to the three men who were awaiting him in the shade of an acacia, he carried a jug filled with blood, another with *era*—milk mixed with water—and a piece of coal. He signaled Kopirkulye to go up to the first jug, whereupon he poured the blood onto the warrior's hands, then his neck and back, saying: "Kopirkulye, take *zombi,* the blood. It is red. When you returned after killing an enemy, you put the desire to kill into the heart of your loved ones. This blood alone can interrupt that problem. Remember always that red puts a stop to evil."

He invited Nweite to come second. He raised the jug of *era* to the warrior's lips and made him drink, saying: "Nweite, drink *era.* It is white. When you returned with another man's cows, you did not see that the ties with their former master were unbroken. Only this *era* can make you the new owner of them. Remember always that white determines ownership."

Finally, Nu-imba ordered Karomeinda to come forth. He blackened the warrior's face, then his chest, with the piece of coal, saying, "Karomeinda, take *tsirkini,* this coal. It is black. When you returned from spreading your curses over the enemy territory, you brought misfortune back with you because you had not defined the limits of its power. Only this coal can keep your own evil curses from befalling you. Remember always that black defines the realm of magic. Go, the three of you, and teach what you have learned to your brothers and your sons." The warriors did so, and their misfortunes ended.

Since then, the Kara-Hamar men and women have used for their person and the decoration of their houses the three magic colors: red, white and black.

1,2. The Hamar ethnic group lives in the south of the province of Gemu Gofa, between Lakes Stephanie and Turkana. This is a region of broad savannas and low mountains covered with acacias and cacti; giant termite nests, occasionally more than 30 feet high, are abundant.

The Kara, who are related to the Hamar ethnic group, are the only sedentary tribe of the region. Their village, Duss, is a large town built on the banks of the Omo River which, 60 miles downstream, empties into Lake Turkana. The round huts are grouped in two quarters separated by a large central square.

1

2

3

4

5

Millet and sorghum granaries stand on a wooden platform which keeps them off the ground. A conical roof, made of intricately plaited rushes, covers the circular walls.

3,4. The women bring up the children and make meals. The Kara usually wear only a skin loincloth, decorated with beads and sea-shells. Their hair is greased with red clay and cut short in a ball shape. Sometimes small balls of clay are worn at the back of the head, in the style of the Bumé, another ethnic group which lives a little lower on the right bank of the river. The Hamar women wear long, very elegant dresses of pelts, ornamented with a profusion of seashells, metal and pearls. Their long, Egyptian style coiffure, also dyed with red clay, falls onto impressive necklaces.

5. In December-January, at the height of the hot season when the drought strikes a se-vere blow, a group of Hamar women arrive in the village of Are Bore where they have heard that rice will be distributed.

1,2,3. Men and women share the work in the fields, depending on ritual considerations. The women prepare the soil by digging and weeding, while the men are responsible for planting seeds, sowing the soil according to sexual symbolism. On the other hand, the harvest is considered to be the birth of the children of the earth and man (the woman playing a kind of midwife rôle) and it is the work of the entire community, men and women alike.

1

2

3

4. While the Kara, living on the banks of the Omo, have no water problems, the situation is quite different for the Hamar, who live a nomadic existence in the arid zones. During the hot season, the smallest marsh in the swamps around the lakes is a source of life, despite the parasites that thrive there.

1. *The Kara hairstyle is very elaborate. A part is made from one ear to the other. The front portion is made into braids which frame the forehead. The rest of the hair is drawn back into a thick chignon and held firmly by a colorful cap of glazed earth. Sometimes the Kara glue pieces of bark onto the cap; holes are made in the bark so as to attach feathers to it (photos 1 and 3, page 234).*

1

2

2. *The Kara are very tall. It is not rare to meet some who are over 7 feet. This man is 7 feet, 6 inches. He has rubbed his body with* mor, *animal grease, and cooled himself with water. Then he covers himself with cinders as protection from mosquitoes and the tsetse fly, which devastates animals and men.*

3. *The exceptional beauty of the Hamar women is known throughout East Africa. Emissaries sent by rich families in Ethiopia, Kenya, the Sudan and even faraway Tanzania come to propose marriage. The father of this young woman, who married an important village chieftain, received forty-two cows in return for his daughter. That is considered a veritable fortune here. The necklace she is wearing shows that she is her husband's first wife. A man can have three or four wives, but the first is always the most important in the home.*

3

1. Some Hamar women cover their face with the same red clay they use on their hair.

2,3. The Hamar men are very appearance-conscious. They love anything that shines and can be worn as bracelets, earrings and rings.

3,4. Like all men in this part of Africa, the Hamar and Kara always bring a small wooden stool with them. They also use this as an elbow rest and a useful headrest for sleeping without disturbing their handsome coiffure.

1

2

3

4

1. *The extreme dryness of the climate and the frequent dust clouds blown up by the wind cause widespread conjunctivitis, sometimes leading to partial or total blindness.*

2. *These women are watching the men perform a dance to thank the river for having deposited its fertile silt on the banks. Some are wearing gourds on their head as protection from the blazing sun. In addition to the Hamar and Kara women, others are present from the Bana tribe (recognizable by the untanned skins they wear on their shoulders and over the chest).*

1

2

3

4

5

3,4,5. *Just before the sowing season in October, and just after the January harvest, the Kara organize lengthy festivals with dancing, ritual and secular games. These are also occasions for contracting marriage.*

The men cover their entire bodies (except for the hands and feet) with a white paste made from ashes (supposed to confer virility) mixed with fat. The women adorn themselves with beads, necklaces and leather bands studded with seashells.

The dance begins with singing. Then the men start to jump and hop forward in a row. Hopping higher and higher, they form a circle, occasionally broken, to the accompaniment of the women's excited cries. Later, young unmarried women join the dance and it becomes a sort of "love parade." The girls tease the men they fancy for a husband by ritual movements and suggestive postures— to which the men respond, rather more crudely.

N'MADI

Mauritania

The N'madi do not form an ethnic group in the strict sense of the term. They are the remnants of a caste that is disappearing from the tribal society of Mauritania. It is impossible to trace their history to a common ancestor. Nonetheless, the Mauritanian government recognizes the N'madi as a tribe; its chieftain is remunerated, as are other tribal chiefs in this immense West African nation.

In Berber Arabian dialect, N'madi means hunter. It seems that several centuries ago, perhaps before or during the time of the Songhai Empire, certain clans for various reasons separated from their original tribal groups —more precisely, from those which lived north of the seaport Nouadhibou. They joined together to form a caste apart in the hierarchised society of the Moors. In order to survive, they learned to become expert hunters, utilizing wild desert dogs, developing their own training methods. Puppies are taken hunting with experienced adult dogs; when an animal is caught and slain, the puppy's muzzle and belly are smeared with its blood. Later the puppy learns to capture game and refrain from killing it until its master arrives.

Throughout the years, new members have joined the N'madi community of exiles, which has grown in strength and solidarity. It is ironic that today, just when they have formed the basis of a genuine ethnic group, having remained uncrossed with other strains for many generations, their survival is endangered by two implacable threats: the disappearance of game due to drought (there has been no rainfall in their territory for fourteen years!), and relentless efforts by the Islamic government to integrate all marginal societies into the "official norm."

The N'madi tend to be viewed with contempt by other tribes. They are extremely poor, possessing practically nothing aside from their famous hunting dogs. The government is trying to persuade them to settle near the towns of Oualâta, Tichit, and Bassikounou. As a matter of fact, they have almost always lived in that region, but as nomads, on the high plateau. The tableland over which they roam is a huge sandstone cliff, the Dhar Tichit which 3,500 years ago formed the northern bank of the great salt lake Aouker. It is now a jumble of old stones, ruins of villages, fortifications, tombs—an extraordinary evocation of the Neolithic period of the Stone Age. Earlier populations were undoubtedly obliged to abandon the region as it dried up.

As citizens of Mauritania, the N'madi have adopted the Muslim religion —in their fashion. For example, contrary to Islamic law, their women enjoy considerable freedom; they own family property, the tent they live in, the sheep they raise; they are responsible for bringing up the children; their advice is sought and heeded by the men. Dietary laws and traditional religious restrictions are disregarded.

Sad to say, only two or thee hundred members of this tribe survive on their desert plateau, totally ignored and forgotten.

Masters of the Hounds

As night fell, Zbeida stared at the high mountain, half white sand, half black rock, which soared above him. He'd been warned that only the *jnoun,* the devils, lived there and that he should never ever camp nearby. But nightfall had caught him by surprise, and he had no choice but to pitch his tent at the foot of the mountain. He laid his weapons next to his dromedary and lit a fire. Soon it was night . . . and a young woman appeared, dressed entirely in black. In her hands she held a gourd filled with milk, which she offered to the traveler. Zbeida drank, and as he drank he observed the silent woman from the corner of his eye. She was extraordinarily beautiful, and her eyes glowed strangely in the dark. He was suddenly seized by a violent desire. But he controlled himself and let no sign betray his feelings. With lowered head, he returned the empty gourd to the strange woman, who pretended to leave. Zbeida turned around to get a better view of her, but all he could see were two fiery, glowing eyes observing him. Terrified, he heard a husky voice whisper: "Zbeida, you are very foolish. Not only have you troubled the rest of the *jnoun* despite all warnings, but you dare to lust after one of us! Fortunately for you, you were able to control your impure thoughts. Therefore, this time, and just this once, you will not be punished. But you must leave at dawn and never more, even from afar, must you set eyes upon the black and white mountain."

Thereupon the glowing eyes vanished in the night and Zbeida fell into a sleep as deep as death itself. The next morning, he hastened to decamp. For many months he never returned to that accursed place. However, in time he became increasingly convinced that he had only been dreaming. He was haunted by the memory of that mysterious beautiful woman. Determined to settle the matter once and for all, he decided to return to the devils' mountain. Night was falling when he reached the spot of his previous encampment. Hardly had he dismounted when he was enveloped by a dense, howling sandstorm. When it had passed, Zbeida, crazed and blinded, wandered in the boundless desert. A dog that had come down from the mountain followed him silently . . .

At the same time, in the mountains to the south, D'gagi and his family were fighting the marauding R'yan and Javran tribes. The latter wished to seize the only water in the region, a lake next to which D'gagi's village was built. Despite the stubborn resistance of the defenders, the bandits quickly gained control of half the lake

and the villagers' situation seemed desperate. D'gagi, who had long known how to speak to the *jnoun,* decided to call on them for help. He made a pact with them. The devils would help the villagers to vanquish the bandits; in compensation, D'gagi promised to turn over half of the enemy prisoners to them. The moment the pact was concluded, the part of the water held by the enemy turned to blood; they were thirsty and afraid. Not a single drop of water to drink, and the blazing sun getting hotter and hotter! On the third day, they were forced to surrender.

D'gagi ordered them to advance in groups of four. Two could drink the pure lake water immediately, while the other two would have to enter a house surrounded by a fence, situated outside the village. The bandits obeyed without a word. Half of them drank and became slaves. The other half entered the house and were never seen again, because the *jnoun* were waiting for them there. The devils thus acquired a soul.

But not every single one of them! One of the captives, suspecting a trap, managed to escape. The *jnoun* who had been deprived of his prisoner complained to D'gagi, who could, alas!, do nothing about it.

"D'gagi, you have not kept your word! You have betrayed me! You will be punished for cheating me!" Whereupon a dense, howling sandstorm fell upon the unfortunate man. When the dust had settled, D'gagi, crazed and blinded, wandered in the infinite desert. A dog appeared from nowhere and followed him silently at a distance . . .

Time went on and on and on. Zbeida and D'gagi grew old, but the dog still followed them, relentless witness to their punishment. One day Zbeida lay down exhausted near a bush, bared the nape of his neck to the sun, and waited for death to come. Not far from there, D'gagi, whom fate had led to the same place, did the same. Suddenly the torrid desert air echoed with the voice of the master of good spirits, the lord of the L'gueta: "Zbeida and D'gagi, arise. Your suffering is over, but you will never be reunited with your families. Join together and live by hunting. The devil's two dogs will help you. Everything the first dog meets will lie down before him, so you will call him Batha; the second will bite the heels of his prey to prevent it from escaping, so you will call him Argab. So be it." And thus it was.

Since then, the N'madi have known how to train the devil's dogs to help them hunt game in the desert.

1,2,3. The eerie territory of the N'madi is an immense desert of dunes surrounding the town of Tichit (1), plains, rocky plateaus and a sandstone cliff (2), shown here during a sandstorm. This cliff 3,500 years ago was the northern bank of the great Lake Aouker, now completely dry.

3

1,2. When they decide to stop for a time—particularly in summer, when they camp close to water holes—the N'madi construct a framework of pieces of wood tied together by bits of fabric. The shelter is made high enough for a man to pass upright under the ridgepole branch. Over the top, they stretch a covering made of assorted cloths salvaged along the route of their travels. Wood is so rare in these desolate parts that when they leave they are obliged to take the bits of wood and branches with them to build other shelters farther on.

2

1

3

3. When the N'madi travel and are only concerned with constructing a temporary shelter, they simply hang the tent cloth on sticks. Standing upright in such a shelter is impossible. This family had the chance to trade a magnificent tent covering to the members of another tribe in exchange for a collection of cut stone hatchets, flint arrowheads, and polished pebbles found in the sand. The bareheaded man in the center displays their new treasures.

The N'madi live on Dhar Tichit, the immense plateau that extends for more than 480 miles from Tidjikdja to Oualasta. This area is one of the most extraordinary prehistoric sites of the Sahara. Here, about 3,000 to 4,000 years ago, a population of 300,000 people developed an advanced neolithic culture, vestiges of which may be found throughout the area.

1,2. N'madi means hunters. Although game has practically disappeared because of the increasingly severe drought, the N'madi continue to hunt and sometimes bag jerboas and a few rare antelopes. For this they use dogs called "devil's dogs," whose origin is uncertain. They most likely descend from wild or feral greyhounds.

3,4,5. Puppies are trained for hunting by taking them out in the company of experienced dogs to learn how to spot and scent game. When an animal is caught and slain,

1

2

3

4

5

the puppy's muzzle and belly are smeared with its blood. The puppy is also made to lie down with a flock of sheep, making sure he does not bite them. Thus he learns the difference between game and herd. Gradually, through punishment and rewards (caresses), the puppy learns to chase and corner his prey until his master arrives without killing it. Some hunters own a rifle (5), but the N'madi are so poor that they often have only a heavy stick with which to bludgeon the animal their dogs have caught.

1,3,6,7. *To protect themselves from the rigors of the desert climate, the women wear veils of a material that has been impregnated with indigo, then pressed with a hot iron to give it the shiny aspect of carbon paper. As the indigo rubs off onto their faces, arms and hands, it gives them a strange bluish complexion.*

Women are at least the equals of men. Without going so far as the matriarchy of the Targui clans, N'madi women enjoy great freedom (including freedom of speech), and are the guardians of family traditions and rights. Very elegant, they are also inclined to have a nagging disposition.

1

2

3

4

5

6

4. Women are generally responsible for preparing the kesra *(wheat cakes). The grain is first ground on a millstone; water and salt are added and the resulting dough is kneaded, then covered with hot ashes and sand. Half an hour later, the* kesra *is ready to be eaten.*

2. For hunting expeditions, men wear special garments that have been smeared with the blood of their prey and stored among its pelts in order to acquire its odor. These clothes, of course, are never cleaned.

5. Like many desert tribesmen, N'madi men usually wear a light blue or white boubou and cover their head with a variation of the taguelmoust, *a turban made from long strips of woven cloth stitched together, dyed with indigo and shined with a hot iron, like their women's veils.*

When the men aren't hunting or watching over their meager flocks of goats and sheep, which are their only riches, they love to dance to the rhythm of drums and the clapping of the hands of the women.

Definitions and Tables

Often, words with a real or seemingly scientific connotation are perceived so generally by the non-specialist that they lose the precision which is the very object of scientific terminology. Therefore, I think it is useful to define certain terms used in the present work.

The populations of the earth all belong to the species *Homo sapiens,* but they are classified into clans, lines, tribes, ethnic groups and races, from the smallest group to the largest.

Clan: A group made up of living beings defined according to a specific parental system, whose origins can be traced to an ancestor (or a group of ancestors) who is distinct but who belongs to the realm of myth. (This does not facilitate a precise genealogy.) A clan can be self-sufficient and thus become a political entity in itself, or it can associate with other clans to form a tribe.

Line: A group composed of living beings according to a precise system of filiation, whose origins can be traced to a definite ancestor (or group of ancestors) belonging to the real world. This facilitates a clear, uninterrupted genealogy. The system of lines represents an effective and autonomous group outside the organization of the state.

Tribe: The largest social unit after a clan and a line, articulated genealogically according to a specific parental system (matrilinear or, most often, patrilinear). The tribe occupies its own territory, under the authority of a single head recognized by all its members. Very schematically, the tribe is the intermediary state between the socially non-integrated primitive group and the civilized state.

In the present work, the term *tribe* is often used in place of the term *ethnic group,* as is the custom today in everyday speech.

Ethnic group: A natural grouping of individuals of the same race, designating an often heterogenous population included under the same name depending on sociocultural and occasionally body characteristics.

Race: The natural grouping of human beings with a set of common hereditary physical characteristics. The grouping does not account for the customs, nationalities and languages of the populations involved.

Of all the terms defined above, the term "race" is undoubtedly the one which, in the public understanding, corresponds most closely to its apparent reality. But once the concept of race is accepted as being of biological nature, the notion quickly becomes complex.

1. Primary Races and Secondary Races

Scientists use a hierarchical classification of races. Besides the four primary races, there are twenty-seven secondary races. A primary race is a theoretical unity defined by a system of precise and ideal parameters. The secondary race is composed of a group of populations none of which reveals all the parameters of the primary race; each, however, shows the most common characteristics of the primary race. These are ethno-geographic groups whose definition and outlines are less exact than those of the primary races. In fact, the secondary races come from a mixture of populations who have been brought together as a result of migrations or isolation.

Nevertheless, the study of the variations in protein levels and chromosome patterns of human beings has in recent years revealed astonishing relationships which help illuminate all these problems. The biochemical approach to genetics is making the comparative exploration of blood groups possible, and this is leading us to reconsider established notions regarding ethnic groups and secondary races in particular—for example, the exact origin of the Olmecs, the Eskimos, or the American Indians.

Indeed, we are witnessing the budding of a new genealogical tree—but one that is not yet at cross-purposes with the original division of the four primary races which satisfies many scientists.

PRIMARY RACES	SECONDARY RACES
Australoid	*Australian*
(Homo sapiens	*Vedda*
australasicus, Berg 1825)	
Caucasoid	*Nordic*
or white	*Eastern European*
(Homo sapiens albus,	*Alpine*
Gmelin 1788)	*Dinaric*
	Anatolian
	Turanian
	Mediterranean
	Southern Oriental
	Indo-Afghan
	Ainu
Mongoloid or	*Uralian*
Xanthochroid	*Northern Mongolian*
(Homo sapiens asiaticus,	*Central Mongolian*
Lime 1758)	*Southern Mongolian*
	Indonesian
	Polynesian
	Eskimo
	American Indian
Negroid or	*Melano-African*
Melanoderm (black)	*Ethiopian*
(Homo sapiens	*Negrillo*
afer, Lime 1758)	*Khoisan*
	Melano-Indian
	Melanesian
	Negrito

2. Formation of the Human Races

The formation of the human races conforms to the same laws as those which govern the formation of the other races of the animal kingdom—mutation, selection and adaptation. While the scientific community is in agreement on the first principle, it is divided on the way in which the three laws converged in man. Thus the theory of polyphyletism, which takes particular note of the immense diversity of the human populations, holds that the four great traditional races arose from independent sources which had already been genetically differentiated and determined before the appearance of the human species from the species which preceded man. This theory has been abandoned following further studies in anatomy and paleontology.

Today, anthropologists unanimously agree that the four races descended from a common genealogical tree which appeared in East Africa about three million years ago. The diversity of the human races and sub-races is explained by the following three phenomena:

Domestication: Comparative studies in zoology show that the domestication of animals leads to the preservation of genetic mutations which have been progressively acquired over the generations. They seem to disappear in the wild state because of natural selection. Thus, the appearance of a number of domestic races can be observed alongside one or several wild species. An example of this is the wolf compared to the great numbers of canine races. The same is true for the domesticated man, with the appearance of progressively acquired physical mutations brought about by cultures, habitats, customs and techniques.

Migrations: The great migrations of prehistory, followed by the movements of populations due to conquests, famine and the climate, first brought about the population of the entire earth and then the intermingling of the various races.

Isolation: After the phenomenon of migration came that of isolation. Isolated populations are those which, at some given time following natural changes such as glaciation periods or geophysical shifts, become immobilized and isolated in a region. Natural selection and the particular influence of different surroundings probably accentuated and ensured genetic mutations in these cases. It is believed that the differentiation of the great primary races came between the two last glaciation periods.

Ethnolinguistic Classification

Some ethnic groups became disproportionately large when they entered the so-called civilized state, and a great number of them today are indistinguishable. On the other hand, others have died out, or else they are languishing or even regressing. Classifying them poses the following problems:

– Classifying the populations of the world using exclusively social criteria today seems questionable.

– It has become apparent that the assignment of cultural or religious areas to these populations does not correspond to objective reality.

– Seeking the common ancestor of a given group is often a matter of fantasy.

– Discussing tribes—or, more correctly, vanishing ethnic groups—produces grave contradictions among rival schools of thought. No one agrees on the number, the place, or even the definition of such a concept!

Scientists generally agree on a set of historico-cultural notions based on the comparative study of languages. Linguistic reality does not correspond systematically to geographic or ethnic reality, and vice versa. All English speakers do not live in England, and all the inhabitants of India do not speak Hindi or belong to the same ethnic group. The closer the ethnic group is to its origins and the more faithful it has remained to its customs, the more likely it is to stick to its linguistic identity.

This book is about primitive ethnic groups on the verge of becoming extinct in the near future—if this is not already so for some of them. I think that there is merit in using an ethnolinguistic classification within a broad general context. In addition, the complexity of the linguistic tables, on which the international scientific community in fact is in agreement, will demonstrate the difficulty of grouping and classifying all the world's ethnic groups.

A lot of time and effort was required for linguists alone to agree more or less on a classification system. When ethnologists, historians and biochemists participated in these discussions, it is easy to imagine the number of problems that came forth.

Human migrations

Red: Homo erectus *(1 million years* B.C.*)*
Blue: Homo sapiens *(40,000 to 10,000 years* B.C.*)*

Preliminary Note

The following tables indicate the groups existing today. All groups which became extinct in ancient times, or recently (the Hittites or Yaghans, for example) have been excluded from this panorama, which is designed simply to give the reader an overall view—one that is as faithful as possible—of today's ethnolinguistic distribution.

Linguistic Complex (Phylum and/or Branches)

This is the final result of the grouping of the various families, considered independently. A complex can be subdivided into branches.

Phylum: a group of languages whose basic vocabulary contains between 12 percent and 1 percent of borrowed words.

Macrophylum: a group of languages whose basic vocabulary contains less than 1 percent of borrowed words.

Microphylum: a group of languages whose basic vocabulary contains between 36 percent and 12 percent of borrowed words.

Linguistic Family

This is the association of closely related groups having the same origin and showing enough analogous characteristics to be grouped together. A family can be subdivided into branches.

Linguistic Group

Called also a basic group, this is the association of closely related elements with the same origin and related characteristics, to such an extent that it is only reasonable to classify them under the same heading.

Linguistic Sub-group

A subdivision of the former, based on the presence of even closer criteria of relationship.

Number of Ethnolinguistic Units

We have chosen not to go beyond sub-groups.

The tables presented here were compiled from research carried out by linguists, ethnologists, and scientists, all of whom cannot be indicated here. However, we should like to acknowledge our principal sources:

BAUMANN, H.	LEACH, E. R.
BEELER, M. S.	LEENHARDT, M.
BENEDICT, P. K.	LÉVI-STRAUSS, C.
BENVENISTE, E.	LI, FANG-KUEI
BOUDA, K.	LONGACRE, R. E.
BRUGMANN, K.	MALINOWSKI, B.
BRYAN, M. A.	MASON, J. A.
CAPELL, A.	MEAD, M.
COWAN, H.K.J.	MEILLET, A.
DUMEZIL, G.	MÉTRAUX, R.
DURKHEIM, E.	PINNOW, H. J.
DYEN, I.	RAY, S. H.
FRAZER, A.	SAPIR, E.
FREEMAN, J. D.	SHAFER, R.
GRACE, G. W.	SOUSTELLE, J.
GREENBERG, J. H.	SWADESH, M.
GRIAULE, M.	TAILLARDAT, J.
HAAS, M. R.	THURNWALD, R.
HAMP, E. P.	TOSCHI, P.
HAUDRICOURT, A. G.	VENDRYES, J.
HAUDRY, J.	VOEGELIN, C. F.
JACOBSON, R.	VOEGELIN, F. M.
KEY, H.	WESTPHAL, E.O.J.
KEY, M.	WILLIAMSON, K.
KRISHNAMURTI, B. H.	WURM, S. A.
LANTERNARI, V.	Z'GRAGGEN, J. A.

* = not classifiable as a group
** = not classifiable as a family

ENSEMBLE	BRANCH		FAMILY	GROUP	UNITS	LOCATION
GE-PANO-CARIB	GE-BORORO (macrophylum)		BORORO		2	BRAZIL
		macro-GE	BOTOCUDO		2	BRAZIL
			CARAJA		3	BRAZIL
			CAINGANG		1	BRAZIL. PARAGUAY
			GE	ACROA	4	BRAZIL
				ACUA	2	BRAZIL
				CAYAPO	9	BRAZIL
				HOTI	11	BRAZIL
				*	2	BRAZIL
			MACHACALI		2	BRAZIL
			NAMBICUARA		3	BRAZIL
	CARIB (macrophylum)		CARIB	NORTHERN	28	BRAZIL. COLOMBIA. GUIANA. VENEZUELA
				NORTHWESTERN	8	COLOMBIA. VENEZUELA
				SOUTHERN	9	BRAZIL
			PEBA-YAGUAN		2	BRAZIL. COLOMBIA
			WITOTOAN		7	COLOMBIA
	PANOAN (macrophylum)		GUAYCURÚ		2	ARGENTINA
			MATACO	MATACO	4	ARGENTINA. PARAGUAY
				MACA	1	PARAGUAY
			PANO-TACANA	PANO	12	BRAZIL. PERU
				TACANA	27	BOLIVIA. PERU
			**		1	ARGENTINA
CHIBCHAN (macrophylum)	CHIBCHAN (microphylum)		CHIBCHAN	EASTERN	4	COLOMBIA
				PACIFIC	3	COLOMBIA. PANAMA
				WESTERN	8	COSTA RICA. PANAMA
			MISUMALPAN		3	HONDURAS. NICARAGUA
			WAICAN		2	BRAZIL. VENEZUELA
			**		3	GUATEMALA. HONDURAS. SALVADOR
	PAEZ (microphylum)		BARBACOAN	CAYAPO-COLORADO	2	ECUADOR
				PASTO	5	COLOMBIA
			CHOCO		3	COLOMBIA
			INTERANDINE	COCONUCAN	3	COLOMBIA
				PAEZ	2	COLOMBIA
			JIRARAN		2	VENEZUELA
			**		3	BOLIVIA. BRAZIL. VENEZUELA
ALGONQUIAN (macrophylum)			ALGONQUIAN		14	CANADA. UNITED STATES
			MUSKOGEAN		5	UNITED STATES
			? CHEMAKUAN		1	UNITED STATES
			? KUTENAI		1	CANADA. UNITED STATES
			? SALISH		15	CANADA. UNITED STATES
			? WAKASHAN	KWAKIUTLAN	2	CANADA
				NOOTKAN	2	CANADA. UNITED STATES
			? YUROK-WIYOT		2	UNITED STATES
HOKALTECAN (phylum)			PALAIHNIHAN		1	UNITED STATES
			POMO		3	UNITES STATES
			TEQUISTLATECAN		2	UNITED STATES
			TLAPANECAN		1	UNITED STATES
			YUMAN	DELTA CALIFORNIAN	2	UNITED STATES
				PAÏ	2	UNITED STATES
				**	2	UNITED STATES
			**		4	MEXICO. UNITED STATES
OTO-MANGUEAN (phylum)			CHINANTECAN		7	MEXICO
			MIXTECAN		6	MEXICO
			OTOMI-PAME	NORTHERN	2	MEXICO
				CENTRAL	2	MEXICO
				SOUTHERN	2	MEXICO
			OLMECAN	POPOLOC	3	MEXICO
				MAZATEC	1	MEXICO
			ZAPOTECAN		2	MEXICO

AMERICA

ENSEMBLE	BRANCH		FAMILY	GROUP	SUB-GROUP	UNITS	LOCATION
SIOUAN (macrophylum)			CADDOAN			3	UNITED STATES
			IROQUOIAN	CHEROKEE		1	UNITED STATES
				NORTHERN		4	CANADA. UNITED STATES
			SIOUAN	CROW-HIDATSA		3	UNITED STATES
				MISSISSIPPI VALLEY		4	UNITED STATES
				✶✶		2	UNITED STATES
AZTEC-TANOAN (phylum)			KIOWA-TANOAN			4	MEXICO. UNITED STATES
			UTO-AZTECAN	NAHUATLAN		2	GUATEMALA. HONDURAS. MEXICO. SALVADOR
				SHOSHONEAN		4	UNITED STATES
				SONORAN		7	MEXICO. UNITED STATES
				LUISEÑO-CAHUILLA		2	MEXICO
ANDEAN-EQUATORIAL (phylum)	ANDEAN	ANDEAN I	CHON			2	ARGENTINA
			✶✶			3	ARGENTINA. CHILE. ECUADOR
		ANDEAN II	QUECHUMARAN			2	BOLIVIA. ECUADOR. PERU
		ANDEAN III	CAHUAPANAN			2	PERU
			ZAPAROAN			2	ECUADOR. PERU
		ANDEAN IV	✶✶			5	BOLIVIA. CHILE. ECUADOR
	EQUATORIAL		ARAWAKAN	ARAUÁN		9	BRAZIL. PERU
				CHAPACURA-WANHAMAN		12	BRAZIL. BOLIVIA
				MAIPURAN		81	BRAZIL. BOLIVIA
			CARIRI			2	BRAZIL
			CUICA-TIMOTE			2	VENEZUELA
			GUAHIBO-PAMIGUAN	GUAHIBO		2	COLOMBIA
				PAMIGUAN		2	COLOMBIA. VENEZUELA
			MOCOA			1	COLOMBIA
			PIAROAN			3	VENEZUELA
			TUPI	TUPARI		5	BRAZIL
				TUPI-GUARANI		18	ARGENTINA. BRAZIL. COLOMBIA. FRENCH GUIANA. PERU
				YURUNA		1	BRAZIL
				✶		1	BRAZIL
			YURACAREAN			2	BOLIVIA
			ZAMUCOAN			2	BOLIVIA. PARAGUAY
			✶✶			2	BOLIVIA. PERU
	JIVAROAN					3	ECUADOR. PERU
	macro-TUCANOAN		PUINAVE			2	BRAZIL
			CATUQUINA			16	BRAZIL
			TUCANOAN			11	BRAZIL. COLOMBIA. ECUADOR. PERU
			✶✶			5	BRAZIL. BOLIVIA. VENEZUELA
PENUTIAN (phylum)			CHINOOK			2	UNITED STATES
			CHIPAYAN			2	BOLIVIA. PERU
			MAIDU			3	UNITED STATES
			MAYAN	CHOLAN		3	MEXICO
				HUASTECAN		2	MEXICO
				KANHOBALAN		2	GUATEMALA
				MAMEAN-IXILIAN		2	GUATEMALA. MEXICO
				QUICHEAN		6	GUATEMALA. HONDURAS. PANAMA. SALVADOR
				TZELTALAN		3	MEXICO
			MIWOK-COSTANOAN			2	UNITED STATES
			MIXE-ZOQUEAN			6	MEXICO
			SAHAPTIN-NEZ PERCÉ			2	UNITED STATES
			TOTONACAN			4	MEXICO
			WINTUN			2	UNITED STATES
			YOKUTS			1	UNITED STATES
			✶✶			5	ARGENTINA. UNITED STATES. MEXICO. CHILE
NA-DENE (phylum)	ATHABASCAN-EYAK		ATHABASCAN	ATHABASCAN	NORTHERN	18	UNITED STATES
					PACIFIC COAST	4	UNITED STATES
					APACHEAN	2	UNITED STATES
				EYAK		1	UNITED STATES
			✶✶			2	CANADA. UNITED STATES

ENSEMBLE	FAMILY	GROUP	SUB-GROUP	UNITS	LOCATION
NIGERIAN-KORDOFANIAN	KORDOFANIAN	KATLA		2	SUDAN
		KOALIB		8	SUDAN
		TALODI		5	SUDAN
		TEGALI		5	SUDAN
		KADUGLI-KRONGO		9	SUDAN
	NIGER-CONGO	ADAMAWA-EASTERN (phylum)	ADAMAWA	57	CAMEROON. CENTRAL AFRICAN REPUBLIC. CHAD. CONGO. NIGERIA
			EASTERN	29	CAMEROON. CENTRAL AFRICAN REPUBLIC. CONGO. SUDAN. ZAIRE
		BENUE-CONGO (phylum)	BANTOID	557	ANGOLA. BOTSWANA. CABINDA. CAMEROON. CONGO. MALAWI. MOZAMBIQUE. NIGERIA. SUDAN. TANZANIA. ZAMBIA. ZIMBABWE
		CONGO	CROSS RIVER	47	NIGERIA
			JUKUNOID	104	CAMEROON. NIGERIA
			PLATEAU	89	NIGERIA
		WEST ATLANTIC	NORTHERN	31	BURKINA FASO. CAMEROON. CHAD. GAMBIA. GUINEA. MALI. MAURITANIA. NIGERIA. SENEGAL. SIERRA LEONE
			SOUTHERN	16	GUINEA. SIERRA LEONE
			*	1	GUINEA
		GUR	KIRMA-TYURAMA	2	IVORY COAST
			LOBI	8	BURKINA FASO. IVORY COAST. GHANA.
			SENOUFO	11	BURKINA FASO. IVORY COAST. GHANA. MALI
			CENTRAL GUR	46	BURKINA FASO. IVORY COAST. DAHOMEY. GHANA. TOGO
			*	6	BURKINA FASO. IVORY COAST. DAHOMEY. MALI. NIGERIA. TOGO
		KWA	CENTRAL AKOKO	2	NIGERIA
			EDO	17	NIGERIA
			EWE	2	DAHOMEY. GHANA. TOGO
			GÃ-ADANGME	2	DAHOMEY. GHANA. TOGO
		IDOMA		6	NIGERIA
			IGBO	3	NIGERIA
			IJO	28	NIGERIA
			KRU	8	IVORY COAST. LIBERIA
			LAGOON	9	IVORY COAST
			NUPE-GBARI	4	NIGERIA
			CENTRAL TOGO	14	BURKINA FASO. GHANA. TOGO
			YORUBA	2	DAHOMEY. NIGERIA
			AKAN	13	DAHOMEY. GHANA. IVORY COAST. TOGO
			*	1	NIGERIA
		MANDE	NORTHERN AND WESTERN	15	BURKINA FASO. GAMBIA. GUINEA. IVORY COAST. LIBERIA. MALI. MAURITANIA. SENEGAL. SIERRA LEONE
			SOUTHERN AND EASTERN	8	BURKINA FASO. GHANA. IVORY COAST. MALI
NOT ESTABLISHED	NILO-SAHARAN (phylum)	CHARI-NILE	BERTA	2	ETHIOPIA. SUDAN
			CENTRAL SUDANIC	34	CHAD. CONGO. CENTRAL AFRICAN REPUBLIC. SUDAN. UGANDA. ZAIRE
			EASTERN SUDANIC	67	ETHIOPIA. KENYA. SUDAN. TANZANIA. ZAIRE
			*	1	ETHIOPIA. SUDAN
		KOMAN		7	ETHIOPIA. SUDAN
		MABAN		4	CENTRAL AFRICAN REPUBLIC. CHAD. SUDAN
		SAHARAN		5	CHAD. LIBYA. NIGER. NIGERIA. SUDAN
		*		2	BURKINA FASO. CHAD. DAHOMEY. MALI. NIGER. NIGERIA. SUDAN
NOT ESTABLISHED	KHOISAN	SOUTH AFRICA KHOISAN	HOTTENTOT	35	ANGOLA. BOTSWANA. SOUTH AFRICA
			!XŪ	3	ANGOLA. BOTSWANA. SOUTH AFRICA
			SOUTHERN KHOISAN	4	BOTSWANA. SOUTH AFRICA
		*		2	TANZANIA

AFRICA

ENSEMBLE	FAMILY	BRANCH	GROUP	SUB-GROUP	UNITS	LOCATION
NOT ESTABLISHED	AFROASIATIC	BERBER	TAMARIGHT-RIFF-KABYL		3	ALGERIA. MOROCCO
			ZENATI		17	ALGERIA. EGYPT. LIBYA. TUNISIA
			*		4	CANARY ISLANDS. MOROCCO. MAURITANIA
		CHADIC	BIU-MANDARA	BATA	9	CAMEROON. NIGERIA
				BURA	5	CAMEROON. NIGERIA
				HIGI	5	CAMEROON
				MATAKAM-MANDARA	9	CAMEROON. CHAD. NIGERIA
				TERA	4	NIGERIA
			CHADO-HAMITIC	AFAWA	8	NIGERIA
				BOLEWA	8	NIGERIA
				HAUSA-GWANDARA	2	NIGER. NIGERIA
				KOTOKO	2	CHAD
				MASA	8	CAMEROON. CHAD
				NGIZIM	6	NIGER. NIGERIA
				PLATEAU	13	NIGERIA
				*	1	NIGERIA
		CUSHITIC	AGAU		4	ETHIOPIA
			EASTERN CUSHITIC	HIGHLANDS	5	ETHIOPIA
				LOWLANDS	13	ETHIOPIA. KENYA
			SOUTHERN CUSHITIC		6	ETHIOPIA. KENYA. TANZANIA
			*		1	ETHIOPIA. SUDAN
		OMOTIC	EASTERN OMOTIC		5	ETHIOPIA
			WESTERN OMOTIC	JANJERO	1	ETHIOPIA
				KEFOID	4	ETHIOPIA
				OMETO-GIMIRA	9	ETHIOPIA
				MAJOID	3	ETHIOPIA
				*	1	ETHIOPIA
		SEMITIC	NORTHERN SEMITIC		1	ISRAEL
			SOUTHERN SEMITIC		3	ETHIOPIA. SAUDI ARABIA. UNITED ARAB EMIRATES (ALGERIA. MOROCCO. TUNISIA)

ASIA

ENSEMBLE	FAMILY	BRANCH	GROUP	SUB-GROUP	UNITS	LOCATION
NOT ESTABLISHED	SINO-TIBETAN	SINO-TIBETAN	CHINESE		8	CHINA
			DHĪMĀLISH		2	INDIA. SIKKIM
			DZORGAISH		6	CHINA
			KAM-TAI	KADAI	4	CHINA. VIETNAM
				KAM-SUI	6	CHINA
				TAI	43	BURMA. LAOS. THAILAND
			MIAO-YĀO	MIAO	1	CHINA. LAOS. THAILAND. VIETNAM
				YĀO	3	BURMA. CHINA. LAOS. THAILAND. VIETNAM
			TIBETAN-BURMESE	BURMESE-LOLO	47	BANGLADESH. BURMA. CHINA. LAOS. THAILAND. VIETNAM
				GYARUNG-MISHMI	32	BANGLADESH. INDIA. NEPAL. SIKKIM. THAILAND
				KAREN	8	BURMA. THAILAND
				NAGA NAGA-KUKI-CHIN	92	BURMA. INDIA
				TIBETAN	2	BHUTAN. NEPAL. SIKKIM. THAILAND. TIBET (CHINA & INDIA)
			*		12	ASSAM. NEPAL. TIBET (CHINA & INDIA)

263

ASIA

ENSEMBLE	FAMILY	BRANCH	GROUP	SUB-GROUP	UNITS	LOCATION
NOT ESTABLISHED	AUSTRO-ASIATIC (phylum)		ASLIAN	SENOIC	3	MALAYSIA
				SEMELAIC	3	MALAYSIA
				JAHAIC	1	MALAYSIA
				JAKUN	3	MALAYSIA
			MON-KHMER	BAHNARIC	32	KAMPUCHEA. LAOS. VIETNAM
				KATUIC	24	KAMPUCHEA. LAOS. VIETNAM
				MONIC	2	BURMA. THAILAND
				PEARIC	5	KAMPUCHEA
				KHMUIC	10	LAOS. THAILAND. VIETNAM
				VIET-MU'ONG	2	VIETNAM
				PALAUNG-WA	9	BURMA. THAILAND. VIETNAM
				*	2	INDIA. KAMPUCHEA
			MUNDA	NORTHERN	6	INDIA
				SOUTHERN	3	INDIA
				*	2	INDIA
			NICOBARESE		6	INDIA

ASIA-OCEANIA

ENSEMBLE	FAMILY	BRANCH	GROUP	SUB-GROUP	UNITS	LOCATION
	AUSTRONESIAN	FORMOSAN-AUSTRONESIAN	? NORTHERN CELEBES		14	INDONESIA
			? SOUTH HALMAHERA WEST NEW GUINEA AUSTRONESIAN		23	IRIAN JAYA. MELANESIAN AREA
			FORMOSAN	ATAYALIC	2	FORMOSA
			AUSTRONESIAN	PAIWANIC TSOUIC	12	FORMOSA
			HESPERONESIAN	CENTRAL AND SOUTHERN CELEBES	48	INDONESIA
				PHILIPPINES	111	PHILIPPINE ISLANDS
				WEST INDONESIAN	55	INDONESIA. KAMPUCHEA. MALAYSIA. MADAGASCAR. VIETNAM
				*	4	INDONESIA. PHILIPPINE ISLANDS
			MOLUCCAN	MOLUCCAN	24	INDONESIA
				EAST INDONESIAN	101	INDONESIA
		OCEANIC	ADMIRALTY-WESTERN-ISLANDS	GROUP I	2	MELANESIAN AREA
				GROUP II	21	MELANESIAN AREA
				*	1	MELANESIAN AREA
			BISMARCK ARCH.		34	MELANESIAN AREA
			LOYALTY ISLANDS		3	MELANESIAN AREA
			MICRONESIAN		7	MELANESIAN AREA
			NEW CALEDONIA	NORTHERN	12	MELANESIAN AREA
				SOUTHERN	9	MELANESIAN AREA
			NORTHEASTERN NEW GUINEA		64	MELANESIAN AREA. PAPUA NEW GUINEA.
			NORTHWESTERN NEW HEBRIDES		4	MELANESIAN AREA
			SOUTHERN NEW HEBRIDES		4	MELANESIAN AREA
			EASTERN OCEANIC	POLYNESIAN	27	MELANESIAN AREA
				EFATE-EPI	5	MALAYSIAN AREA
				GUADALCANAL	14	MALAYSIAN AREA
				MALAITA	13	MELANESIAN AREA
				NORTHERN NEW HEBRIDES	42	MELANESIAN AREA
				*	13	MELANESIAN AREA
			PAPUA		52	MALAYSIAN AREA. PAPUA NEW GUINEA
			SANTA CRUZ		2	MALAYSIAN AREA
			SARMIC	SOBEIC	3	MALAYSIAN AREA
				TARPIC	3	MELANESIAN AREA
			NORTHWESTERN AND CENTRAL SOLOMONS		26	MELANESIAN AREA
			*		2	MELANESIAN AREA

ENSEMBLE	FAMILY	GROUP	SUB-GROUP	UNITS	LOCATION
URAL-ALTAIC	URALIC	FINNO-UGRC	FINNO-LAPPIC	16	FINLAND. NORWAY. SWEDEN. USSR
			PARMIC	2	USSR
			UGRIC	3	HUNGARY. USSR
			VOLGAIC	2	USSR
		SAMOYEDIC		5	USSR
	ALTAIC	JAPANESE-RYUKYUAN	JAPANESE	1	JAPAN
			RYUKYUAN	3	JAPAN
		MONGOL		9	AFGHANISTAN. CHINA. MONGOLIA. USSR
		TUNGUS	NORTHERN	6	USSR
			SOUTHERN	11	USSR
		TURKIC	CENTRAL	4	AFGHANISTAN. USSR
			EASTERN	3	AFGHANISTAN. CHINA. USSR
			NORTHERN	10	USSR
			WESTERN	5	USSR
			SOUTHERN	6	AFGHANISTAN. BULGARIA. IRAN. TURKEY. USSR
			*	1	USSR
		**		1	KOREA
	?DRAVIDIAN	CENTRAL		13	INDIA
		NORTHERN		3	AFGHANISTAN. INDIA. IRAN. PAKISTAN
		SOUTHERN		6	INDIA. SRI LANKA
INDOEUROPEAN	BALTIC			2	USSR
	CELTIC	P. CELTIC		2	FRANCE. UNITED KINGDOM
		Q. CELTIC		2	IRELAND. UNITED KINGDOM
	GERMANIC	NORTHERN		2	DENMARK. FINLAND. IRELAND. NORWAY. SWEDEN
		WESTERN		1	ENGLAND
	GREEK			2	GREECE
	INDIC	DARDIC	KOHISTANI	5	INDIA. PAKISTAN
			CHITRALI	2	INDIA. PAKISTAN
			KUNAR	3	INDIA. PAKISTAN
			SINĀ	3	INDIA. PAKISTAN
			*	2	INDIA. PAKISTAN
		CENTRAL INDIC		7	INDIA
		EASTERN INDIC		3	INDIA
		HIMALAYAN ZONE		3	INDIA. NEPAL
		NORTHWESTERN INDIC ZONE		2	INDIA. PAKISTAN
		SINGHALESE-MALDIVIAN		3	SRI LANKA. MALDIVE ISLANDS
		*		3	INDIA. IRAN. NEPAL. USRR
	IRANIAN		EASTERN	8	AFGHANISTAN. USRR
			WESTERN	13	IRAN. PAKISTAN. TURKEY
		NŪRISTĀNĪ		6	AFGHANISTAN
	ITALIC			8	BULGARIA. FRANCE. GREECE. ITALY. PORTUGAL. ROMANIA. SPAIN
	SLAVIC	EASTERN SLAVIC		3	USSR
		WESTERN SLAVIC		5	CZECHOSLOVAKIA. HUNGARY. POLAND
		SOUTHERN SLAVIC		4	BULGARIA. USSR. YUGOSLAVIA
IBERO-CAUCASIAN	CAUCASIAN	NORTHEASTERN	AVARO-ANDI-DIDO	12	USSR
			LAK-DARGWA	2	USSR
			LEZGHIAN	10	USSR
			VEJNAX	3	USSR
		NORTHWESTERN		2 OR 3	MIDDLE EASTERN STATES. TURKEY. USSR
		SOUTHERN		3	TURKEY. USSR
	BASQUE			1	FRANCE. SPAIN
HYPERBOREAN	CHUKCHEE-KAMCHATKAN			5	USSR
	YENISEI-OSTYAK			1	USSR
	YUKAGHIR			1	USSR
	ESKIMO-ALEUT			6	CANADA. UNITED STATES (ALASKA). USSR
	**			1	USSR

ENSEMBLE	FAMILY	GROUP	SUB-GROUP	UNITS	LOCATION
NOT ESTABLISHED	INDO-PACIFIC	ANDAMANESE		2	ANDAMAN ISLANDS
		BOUGAINVILLE	EASTERN	8	BOUGAINVILLE ISLAND
			WESTERN	4	BOUGAINVILLE ISLAND
		NORTHERN HALMAHERA		12	HALMAHERA ISLAND
		LEFT MAY RIVER		6	PAPUA NEW GUINEA
		LEONARD SCHULTZE RIVER		4	PAPUA NEW GUINEA
		CENTRAL MELANESIAN	SANTA CRUZ	4	SANTA CRUZ REEF
			CENTRAL SOLOMONS	4	SOLOMON ISLANDS
		MOMBERAMO RIVER		11	PAPUA NEW GUINEA
		NEW BRITAIN		7	NEW BRITAIN. NEW IRELAND
		CENTRAL NEW GUINEA	HUON-FINISTERRE	62	PAPUA NEW GUINEA
			EASTERN HIGHLANDS	49	PAPUA NEW GUINEA
			WESTERN HIGHLANDS	11	PAPUA NEW GUINEA
		NORTHERN NEW GUINEA	BOGIA	83	PAPUA NEW GUINEA
			MURIK	6	PAPUA NEW GUINEA
			SENTANI	18	PAPUA NEW GUINEA
			SEPIK	39	PAPUA NEW GUINEA
			TAMI	23	PAPUA NEW GUINEA
			TORRICELLI	39	PAPUA NEW GUINEA
			*	19	PAPUA NEW GUINEA
		NORTHEASTERN NEW GUINEA		33	PAPUA NEW GUINEA
		? SOUTHEASTERN NEW GUINEA	BINANDERE	17	PAPUA NEW GUINEA
			DAGA	13	PAPUA NEW GUINEA
			GOILALA	17	PAPUA NEW GUINEA
			KOIARI	32	PAPUA NEW GUINEA
			MAILU	14	PAPUA NEW GUINEA
			MULAHA	3	PAPUA NEW GUINEA
			TOARIPI	4	PAPUA NEW GUINA
			*	2	PAPUA NEW PAPUA
		SOUTHERN NEW GUINEA	AGÖB	8	PAPUA. NEW GUINEA
			DOLAK ISLAND & SOUTHEASTERN WEST IRIAN	14	PAPUA NEW GUINEA
			GOGODALA	2	PAPUA NEW GUINA
			KIKORI RIVER	11	PAPUA NEW GUINEA
			KIWAI	8	PAPUA NEW GUINEA
			MOREHEAD RIVER	4	PAPUA NEW GUINEA
			ORIOMO RIVER	5	PAPUA NEW GUINEA
		SOUTHWESTERN NEW GUINEA	AWYU	9	PAPUA NEW GUINA
			KUKUKUKU	10	PAPUA NEW GUINEA
			MARIND	7	PAPUA NEW GUINEA
			OK	17	PAPUA. NEW GUINEA
			TIRIO	3	PAPUA NEW GUINEA
			*	1	PAPUA NEW GUINEA
		WESTERN NEW GUINEA	I	19	IRIAN JAYA
			II	8	IRIAN JAYA
			III	4	IRIAN JAYA
			IV	3	IRIAN JAYA
			? GOLIATH	9	IRIAN JAYA
			? ASMAT	10	IRIAN JAYA
		TIMOR-ALOR		4	INDONESIA
		*		34	NEW GUINEA

AUSTRALIA

ENSEMBLE	FAMILY	GROUP	SUB-GROUP	UNITS	LOCATION
AUSTRALIAN (macrophylum)	BUNABAN			2	AUSTRALIA
	BURERAN			2	AUSTRALIA
	DALY	BRINKEN-WOGAITY		6	AUSTRALIA
		MULLUK		4	AUSTRALIA
		*		1	AUSTRALIA
	DJAMINDJUNGAN			4	AUSTRALIA
	DJERAGAN	GIDJIC		3	AUSTRALIA
		MIRIWUNIC		2	AUSTRALIA
	GUNWINGGUAN	GUNWINGGIC		4	AUSTRALIA
		YANGMANIC		3	AUSTRALIA
		*		4	AUSTRALIA
	IWAIDJAN			2	AUSTRALIA
	KARWAN			2	AUSTRALIA
	LARAKIAN			2	AUSTRALIA
	MANGERIAN			2	AUSTRALIA
	MARAN	MARIC/*		3	AUSTRALIA
	NYULNYULAN			4	AUSTRALIA
	PAMA-NYUNGAN	ARANDIC		3	AUSTRALIA
		BANDJALANGIC		2	AUSTRALIA
		DIERIC	KARNA/NGURA/*	7	AUSTRALIA
		DURUBULIC		3	AUSTRALIA
		GIABALIC		2	AUSTRALIA
		KULINIC	KULIN/DRUAL/*	6	AUSTRALIA
		KUMBAINGGARIC		2	AUSTRALIA
		MABUIAGIC		2	AUSTRALIA
		MAYAPIC		3	AUSTRALIA
		MURNGIC	YULNGU/*	10	AUSTRALIA
		NARRINYERIC		3	AUSTRALIA
		NYUNGIC	KANYARA	2	AUSTRALIA
			KARDU	6	AUSTRALIA
			MANTHARDA	3	AUSTRALIA
			MARNGU	3	AUSTRALIA
			MIRNINY	2	AUSTRALIA
			NGARGA	5	AUSTRALIA
			NGAYARDA	6	AUSTRALIA
			NGUMBIN	7	AUSTRALIA
			WATI	2	AUSTRALIA
			YURA	5	AUSTRALIA
			*	2	AUSTRALIA
		PAMA-MARIC	MARI	2	AUSTRALIA
			PAMA	25	AUSTRALIA
			YARA	5	AUSTRALIA
			*	4	AUSTRALIA
		TANGKIK		2	AUSTRALIA
		WAKA-KABIC	MIYAN	2	AUSTRALIA
			THAN	2	AUSTRALIA
			KINGKEL	2	AUSTRALIA
		WAKAYA-WARLUWARIC		2	AUSTRALIA
		WIRADJURIC		6	AUSTRALIA
		YOTAYOTIC		3	AUSTRALIA
		YUIN-KURIC		10	AUSTRALIA
		*		38	AUSTRALIA
	TJINGILI-WAMBAYAN	WAMBAYIC/*		3	AUSTRALIA
		*		1	AUSTRALIA
	WORORAN	UNGARINYNIC		3	AUSTRALIA
		WORORIC		6	AUSTRALIA
		WUNAMBULIC		3	AUSTRALIA
	**			12	AUSTRALIA